To:

_____

From:

_____

Why
Keep Praying

When You Don't
See Results

Robert Morris

THOMAS NELSON
Since 1798

Contents

Introduction

Picture a late afternoon following a long, weary trek along the dusty roads of Palestine. The Teacher and the twelve are looking for a place to get out of the sun and the heat—somewhere to rest a little before resuming their journey in the cool of the evening.

They find a bit of shade under a cluster of palms, near a well. Instead of napping, however, the twelve keep their eyes on the Teacher, who has another story to tell.

And no one wants to miss one of Jesus' stories.

This time He paints a picture of a stubborn cold fish of a judge and his encounter with a vulnerable widow, who had suffered a terrible injustice in her life. This judge, however, couldn't have cared less about the widow and her worries. Time after time he turned her away, unwilling to help her or to make a judgment. But instead of becoming discouraged and accepting this treatment, the widow kept coming back—over and over again—to stand before this hard-as-nails official.

He just wanted her to go away, but she refused.

She refused to let go.

She refused to be put off or become discouraged.

She refused to give up.

She ignored his every attempt at intimidation.

She was there first thing Monday morning, when he opened the doors. She was there again on Tuesday when he looked through his office window. She was back again on Wednesday, ahead of everyone else in line. It was the same on Thursday and Friday and every other day court was in session. She became a fixture of the court, like a lamp or a bench—and he thought he could hear her voice in his sleep.

He had been known as a stubborn man through the years, but he finally realized he had met his match. This widow was just as stubborn as he.

So the judge granted her justice—simply to get rid of her.

If Jesus Christ, God's Son,

needed to pray

and make vital, personal contact

with God the Father *every day,*

do you think there's a possibility

that we need to do that too?

As Jesus told the story, the disciples probably looked at each other with a bit of bewilderment. Were they hearing right? Was He really saying that God was like a cranky judge who couldn't be bothered with "little people" and their problems?

No.

In fact, the star of this drama was the tenacious, single-minded woman who kept pursuing her goals in the face of indifference, hostility, and zero encouragement.

That, said Jesus, is how we need to pray.

And that is the *why* of this story. Luke 18:1 says it explicitly: "Now He was telling them a parable to show that at all times they ought to pray and not to lose heart" (NASB).

Lose heart? That's another way to say "give up."

In the original language, the term for "lose heart" means "to be afraid, to become discouraged, to become weary or tired, to despair, to lose heart, to tire of."[1] Jesus was saying, "Dear friends, I want to encourage you to pray and to keep praying. Don't be afraid. Don't be discouraged. Don't become weary or tired. Don't give in to despair. Keep seeking God because (unlike the cranky old judge in the story) He cares deeply about you and will certainly hear and respond."

Again and again in their journeys, Jesus' followers had watched how He made a priority of prayer. But why did He do that? He was and is the Son of God, equal with God the Father. So why would He invest so much time talking to God?

I believe Jesus prayed because He *needed* to pray.

Someone will ask, "How could God need anything?"

Here's how. When He chose to come to earth, He laid down His divinity and picked up His humanity. As a human being, He needed the power of the Holy Spirit in His life, just as we do. As a human, He needed to hear His Father's voice. He needed to pour out His soul and have fellowship with the Father. He needed strength and guidance and help as He walked on this earth as a human being.

Here's a question for all of us.

If Jesus Christ, God's Son, needed to pray and make vital, personal contact with God the Father every day, do you think there's a possibility that *we* need to do that too?

Absolutely, we do.

We need to pray. And as Jesus' story in Luke 18 tells us, we need to *keep* praying even when it seems like the answer is a million miles away and will never come.

But why did Jesus tell that story anyway? Why did He encourage His followers to make prayer a huge priority in their lives—and why was it important that they refuse to give up or lose heart?

Because He knew what was coming in their lives, and they didn't.

Jesus understood how desperately they would need that warm, personal, living connection with their heavenly Father. Difficult days lay ahead for them, days of testing and trouble. But if they really began to grasp what an immeasurable resource they possessed through the act of prayer, if they learned how to pray and practiced praying persistently, they would be ready for what lay ahead—both the trials and the unimaginable opportunities.

Jesus knows that about you and me too. We don't know what lies ahead of us in the coming days, but He does. We can't see around the bend in our lives, but He can. And He knows we *need* to pray. We need the counsel, perspective, warnings, and companionship of our God now and in the future. We need encouragement to keep praying, even when the answers don't

We need

encouragement to

keep praying,

even when the answers

don't come as quickly as

we had hoped

or don't take the form

or shape we expected.

come as quickly as we had hoped or don't take the form or shape we expected.

In the pages ahead I want to us to think about why we pray at all, what it means to pray and intercede for others, how we can keep that vital line to heaven open and clear, and why we should pray with great patience and persistence, no matter how long it is before we receive His answer.

It's almost a cliché to claim that this or that will change a person's life.

But this really will.

I would stake my life on it.

Chapter 1

Why Pray at All?

Once when I was speaking on prayer in another church, God gave me a word of encouragement for an older woman I met during a break in the service. I'd never seen her before in my life, but I felt strongly that God was leading me to speak to her.

"Ma'am," I said, "here is something the Lord has put on my heart to say: You know how to pray. You know how to intercede. And you need to teach other women how to pray." I heard these words coming out of my mouth, and then God's direction became even more specific. I said to her, "You need to teach women who are married to unbelievers how to pray for their unbelieving husbands to come to Christ."

After the service, the pastor of the church said to me, "I

want you to meet this woman you spoke to and hear her story." So he took me over to her, and she gave me this unforgettable account of God's answer to her intercession.

She lived in Oklahoma and had been married to an unbeliever for forty-two years. Then one day, while traveling in Florida, her husband was killed in a car crash.

About a month after her husband died, this woman received a phone call. A stranger identified himself and asked for her husband by name. "I met him recently," the man on the phone explained, "and we exchanged contact information."

"I'm sorry to tell you this," she replied, "but he recently passed away. He was in a car accident in Florida."

"In Florida?" the man said.

"Yes," she replied, "he was on a business trip."

The man on the other end of the line became very quiet. Then he said, "Ma'am, do you mind my asking you on what day it was—when did he pass away?"

She had no idea where this conversation was heading, but she told him the day.

"Did you talk to your husband that day?" he asked her.

"I did," she replied, "We spoke that morning. He would call me every morning and every evening when he was away on business trips. But then he was . . . killed, and I didn't talk to him that night."

"Ma'am," the man on the phone said, "I'm thinking I have some very good news for you. I'm a believer in Christ and a businessman. I go to work every morning in a suit and tie. But one day—the day your husband died—God began to speak to me in a way I just couldn't shake. I was all dressed up in my suit and tie and ready to drive to work, when He told me to go out to the freeway and *hitchhike.* It seemed strange, but I obeyed Him. I put my thumb out, and the first car that pulled over was your husband's. I led him to Jesus that day, and he was going to call you that night and give you the news."

This was a woman who believed in prayer—even though she hadn't seen any direct results for forty-two years. Like the woman in the Luke 18 story, she kept lining up every morning

She kept lining up
every morning
and every night
in front of God's throne,
presenting her request,
pleading for the salvation
of her husband.

and every night in front of God's throne, presenting her request, pleading for the salvation of her husband.

The months went by. The years went by. But she never quit. She never stopped believing until her husband's dying day. And then, just to encourage her heart, God gave her the news she would have otherwise had to wait until heaven to receive.

I'll never forget that courageous woman's story. It showed me once again how faithful God is to answer the determined, persistent prayers of ordinary people like you and me. It also reminded me that we can trust His timing—even though it may not be *our* timing.

So what is prayer? Prayer is an open door into the presence of our God and Creator, where we can praise Him for who He is, thank Him for His goodness, confess our sins and find forgiveness, and bring our deepest concerns, our silent fears, and our heartfelt desires to place before Him.

Prayer is an invitation for real people to express real needs to a listening, loving Father and experience real, tangible answers. The apostle Paul says it so beautifully in Philippians 4:6–7:

> Don't worry about anything; instead, pray about everything; tell God your needs, and don't forget to thank him for his answers. If you do this, you will experience God's peace, which is far more wonderful than the human mind can understand. His peace will keep your thoughts and your hearts quiet and at rest as you trust in Christ Jesus. (TLB)

Can you imagine the wonder and comfort the Lord's disciples must have felt in the Upper Room when Jesus offered them a way to keep in touch with Him after He left this earth? Jesus assured them that He would be listening and that He would answer their petitions—they simply had to ask in His name.

> And whatever you ask in My name, that I will do, that the Father may be glorified in the Son. If you ask anything in My name, I will do it. (John 14:13–14)

Prayer

is an invitation for real people to express

real needs to a listening, loving Father

and experience real, tangible answers.

You did not choose Me, but I chose you and appointed you that you should go and bear fruit, and that your fruit should remain, that whatever you ask the Father in My name He may give you. (John 15:16)

And in that day you will ask Me nothing. Most assuredly, I say to you, whatever you ask the Father in My name He will give you. Until now you have asked nothing in My name. Ask, and you will receive, that your joy may be full. (John 16:23–24)

Those words are for us just as much as they were for His disciples at the Last Supper. We are invited not only to pray, but also to ask in Jesus' name.

Ask anything in His name.

Ask the Father in His name

Ask, receive, and be joyful.

And why wouldn't we ask? The invitation is in our Bible, the book we call our very own guidebook for life. We claim to believe every word.

So, why don't we pray?

I don't think that most of us consciously make the decision *not* to pray. We don't fold our arms across our chests and say to ourselves, "Well, I just refuse to do this. I'm not going to pray." Yet we make that very decision subconsciously many, many times a day. So many mornings of our lives, we get swept along in the stream of the day's activities and opt not to spend time with God, not to pray to Him, not to ask Him about anything. So many nights before we pull up the covers and go to sleep, we choose to read a book, check our e-mail, prowl the kitchen for a snack, or think through the next day's schedule instead of seeking the mind and presence of our Creator.

Why is that? Why don't we take great delight in speaking with God?

There may be many reasons, but three occur to me right off the top.

If we are
self-satisfied,
we won't feel the need to be
God-satisfied.

We Imagine We Can
Handle Life on Our Own

If we are pleased with ourselves and with our own devices for coping with life, we won't feel the need or inclination to seek the Lord and call out to Him. If we are self-satisfied, we won't feel the need to be God-satisfied. Oh, we might reserve the right to call on Him after we find ourselves in the middle of really big things like death, danger, and disaster. But on most days as life moves along as normal, we think we're doing just fine and don't really need help from the Almighty. So we simply don't bother to call on Him.

For example, the New Testament urges us to pray and intercede "for kings and all those in authority, that we may live peaceful and quiet lives" (1 Timothy 2:2 NIV). But if life is moving along smoothly, we can easily ignore this directive. *Besides,* we ask ourselves, *what good will it really do? What difference will it really make?*

But isn't it amazing how concerned we become when a truly big event threatens to touch our lives in a direct way? A number of years ago, for instance, an angry monster of a storm called Hurricane Katrina devastated a large swath of our country. The weather forecasters had seen it take shape in the Gulf of Mexico and warned us about it. They told us it was coming. But many believers, in my opinion, didn't take the threat seriously enough and didn't pray as much as they might have.

By the way, where do such natural disasters come from? From God? No, I believe that natural disasters are *natural.* We live in a fallen world plagued by many problems, including natural disasters like earthquakes and tornadoes and, yes, hurricanes. Even so, I believe God's people can *turn* natural disasters through prayer. But that didn't happen with Katrina. Too many of us neglected to pray before the storm came blasting into our nation, and it unleashed almost incomprehensible damage.

And then, seemingly days later, another Category 5 superstorm followed in Katrina's terrible wake. As Hurricane Rita approached our shores, we were told the storm could not only endanger many more people, but also devastate oil refineries in and around Houston, leading to ecological disaster and skyrocketing prices.

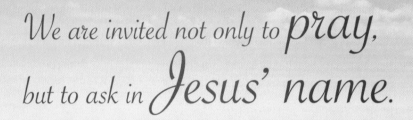

We are invited not only to *pray*, but to ask in *Jesus' name*.

If we really believed that investing time and energy and thought in prayer would actually change things in our lives, wouldn't we spend more time doing just that?

This time many across Texas and the nation really did pray. And Rita turned, not causing anywhere near the damage and loss of life that had been predicted.

Could that have been because we finally turned from our complacency just a little?

We Simply Don't Believe

That may sound a little harsh and a bit difficult to swallow. But if we really believed that investing time and energy and thought in prayer would actually change things, wouldn't we spend more time doing just that?

Think about it. If you *were truly convinced* that spending time in prayer every day for your business would make a significant difference in its success, wouldn't you be inclined to carve out some extra minutes in your day to do it?

If you *knew for sure* that sacrificing some other priorities to pray and seek God's face concerning your marriage could transform your relationship, wouldn't you be willing to make that sacrifice?

If you *accepted beyond all doubt* that crying out to God every day for a child in a season of rebellion would change, soften, alter, or transform that child's character, would you set aside other interests to spend more time in prayer?

Do we really believe that God guides our business decisions, turns our relationships around, or rescues our sons and daughters from the traps of the enemy?

As uncomfortable as I am saying this, I think we sometimes feel that ten minutes in prayer won't really accomplish as much as ten minutes on the Internet, and we make that choice instead.

We really don't believe, right down to the core of who we are, that time invested in prayer will change things.

When it comes to prayer, then, we vote with our actions. If we believe in it, we practice it. If deep down we don't believe it makes a difference, we never seem to find time for it. It will always be an afterthought rather than the most urgent priority of our lives.

We won't be like the widow who camped out in front of the judge's chambers, waiting for him to act. Instead, we'll get discouraged after a short period and walk away.

We Allow Ourselves to Become Discouraged

We may have prayed and prayed and even wept before God for something, and we don't feel like He has answered. So we lose heart. We stop praying. We give up. We do exactly what Jesus warned us *not* to do. In the backwash of our disappointment, we allow the enemy to warp our thinking about prayer.

In the book of Numbers, we read that as the children of Israel were traveling around the land of Edom on the way to the promised land, "the soul of the people became very discouraged on the way. And the people spoke against God" (Numbers 21:4–5). This can happen to any of us if we permit it. We become discouraged on the way and lose our perspective.

When that happened to the Israelites, they turned against God rather than turning *to* Him. They murmured and complained instead of bringing their disappointment to Him and praying about it.

Billy Graham has a better idea. He once wrote: "The Christian life is not a constant high. I have my moments of deep

What inexpressibly wonderful,
life-transforming opportunities are we
missing by not seeking *God* in prayer?

discouragement. I have to go to God in prayer with tears in my eyes, and say, 'O God, forgive me,' or 'Help me.'"[2]

So much for the reasons why we *don't* pray. Why *should* we pray? What inexpressibly wonderful, life-transforming opportunities are we missing by not seeking God in prayer? The two reasons I'd like you to consider also happen to be attributes of God—characteristics of who He is and what He does. These attributes of our Creator should cause us to want to pray more and more.

We Pray Because God Is Sovereign

To say it in the simplest way, *sovereign* means "supreme." When we say that God is sovereign, we are saying that He is the supreme Ruler of the universe. We pray to a sovereign God because He is the supreme Ruler of the universe who can move heaven and earth to help us, provide for us, and fill our lives with purpose and joy.

But many people, I think, have misunderstood and misapplied this truth about God. Some will say, "Sovereignty means that God's going to do whatever He wants to do no matter what, so there's no use in asking Him for anything."

Satan, our enemy, loves to take advantage of that misunderstanding. He will come alongside and whisper, *Why pray? Why even bother? God will do whatever He wants to do anyway.*

In the gospel of Matthew, Jesus tells us, "Your Father knows the things you have need of before you ask Him" (6:8). Sometimes, however, I think we read those words like this: "The Father knows what you need, so don't bother asking. Don't waste your breath." As a result, we become apathetic. We shrug our shoulders. We begin to think of prayer as a religious formality. We lose our sense of urgency, our hope, and we may even slip into cynicism.

But that is not what the sovereignty of God means.

The supremacy of God doesn't mean He will do whatever He wants to do no matter what. This is a misinterpretation of

God's will. People may say (or think) this because they misunderstand the definition of the word *will*.

Let me give you the best one-word definition:

Will = *Desire*

When you draw up a last will and testament, what you are actually saying is, "This is my *desire* for the $83.62 I will leave behind after the bills are paid." That is your will. Your will is your desire.

So what is God's desire? The Bible tells us that quite clearly, Let's look for a moment at 2 Peter 3:9:

> The Lord is not slack concerning His promise, as some count slackness, but is longsuffering toward us, not willing that any should perish but that all should come to repentance.

Did you get that? God *is not willing* that anyone should perish. His will, His strong desire—wider than time and more powerful than a supernova—is that all should come to repentance. Looking closer at the original meaning of that word translated "willing" deepens its resonance. It means that He is not disposed, He is not minded, and it is not His intention that anyone should fall short of salvation. It is *not* His will and *not* His desire that anyone would ever be lost.

But will people be lost?

Yes.

Will all people come to repentance?

Sadly, no. Not even if God desires it.

Why not? Because God in His sovereignty, exercising His will as Supreme Ruler, chose to also give free will to the men and women created in His image.

The reason people perish, then, isn't because of God's will, but rather because of *their* wills. They exercise their wills to refuse God's offer of salvation, and that's why they perish.

"For I know the thoughts that I think toward you, says the LORD, thoughts of peace and not of evil, to give you a future and a hope" (Jeremiah 29:11). God's thoughts are for our good. His thoughts are for every person to come to Christ, and He has provided a way for every person to be saved. That's what He *wills*. What He desires.

His will,

His strong desire——

wider than time

and more powerful

than a supernova——

is that all should

come to repentance.

God can't get better,

because He is already the best.

He is perfect and perfection itself.

And although God in His sovereignty has given us the freedom not to choose His ways, He has also created us in His image, giving us the will to want what He wants. And when we make that desire a part of prayer, amazing things can happen.

When the disciples asked Jesus how they should pray, one of the phrases He gave them was:

> *Your kingdom come.*
> *Your will be done*
> *on earth as it is in heaven. (Matthew 6:10)*

Prayers will be answered in our lives because *our* will moves *God's* will from heaven to earth—all in the context of God's sovereignty.

Now sometimes we will add to our prayers the phrase, "If it be Thy will . . ." (We like to use the old King James English when we say that.) The truth is, however, that there are many areas of life in which we *already know God's will.*

We have, for instance, already seen that it is God's will that no one would be lost. We might pray, "God, if it's Your will, please save my neighbor, Bill." And God might well reply to us, "My will is that you get your will out of that recliner and walk across the street and talk to Bill!"

We Pray Because God Is Changeless

God does not change, will not change, and cannot change. In the book of Malachi, He declares: "For I am the LORD, I do not change" (3:6).

God doesn't change, because if He *could* change, He could get better. But He can't get better, because He is already the best. He is perfect and perfection itself.

Satan knows that truth, too, and has had thousands of years to practice twisting it to his own ends. Referring to the sovereignty of God, he will say, *God will do whatever He wants to do, so it doesn't matter if you pray.* Then switching to God's changelessness, he will say, *You think you can change things through prayer? What a joke. You can't change God's mind, because God can't change. So your prayers are useless. You're running into a brick wall a thousand miles thick, and you'll never move it. You're pushing against Mount Everest, but you'll never make it sway.*

When the Bible says that God is unchangeable, however, it isn't saying that God doesn't change His *mind*. It is saying that God doesn't change His *character.* God cannot and will not change His character. He is who He is. But according to Scripture, He can and will change His mind!

Abraham knew this. In Genesis 18:16–33 we see the patriarch standing before the Lord, actually praying for Sodom and Gomorrah and pleading that the Lord would reconsider His plan to destroy the evil cities. Abraham began by asking the Lord not to wipe out the cities if he found fifty righteous people there. God agreed, but fifty righteous people couldn't be found. So Abraham prayed again. Going back and forth in conversation with God, he gradually worked the number down to just ten.

But there weren't even ten righteous people in either of those dark, unhappy cities, and God did move in judgment against them. But Abraham learned that he could reason with God in prayer—and make a difference. God listens and cares.

Moses knew this as well. And it's a good thing for the Jewish people that he did.

In Exodus 32:9–10, we read that God was on the knife edge of destroying the whole nation and starting over again with Moses. But Moses pleaded with God to turn aside from His intention of judgment and spare the people.

And what happened then? We read that "the LORD relented from the harm which He said He would do to His people" (v. 14).

Could that be right? The Lord, the God of the universe, relented from a course of action that He had planned?

Yes, that's what Scripture says. Another translation puts it even more starkly: "So *the* LORD *changed his mind* about the terrible disaster he had threatened to bring on his people" (NLT, emphasis mine).

But why? Why would He do that? Because Moses prayed. One microscopic dust speck of a human being on one little dust speck of a planet in the vast universe called on the eternal Creator of all to change His mind about the destiny of a nation.

And that's what God did.

One microscopic dust speck of a human being on one
little dust speck of a planet in the vast universe called on
the eternal Creator of all to change His mind about
the destiny of a nation. And that's what God did.

God is immutable

and will **never**, ever change His character.

But He can and will *change*

His mind when His people **pray**.

We can see the same dynamic in the story of Jonah. After his wet-and-wild encounter with the great fish, the runaway prophet did some repenting of his own and set out for Nineveh to deliver the message God had given him: "Yet forty days, and Nineveh shall be overthrown!" (Jonah 3:4)

Did it happen? Was Nineveh destroyed at that time?

No, it wasn't. Not in forty days, and not in forty years. Nineveh remained as a city for possibly one hundred fifty years. Why? Because the people of Nineveh changed their minds about the way they had been living, and God changed *His* mind about destroying them.

God had said it would happen, but it didn't happen. The threatened judgment didn't fall, and that nearly drove Jonah crazy. He hated the people of Nineveh (for many logical and understandable reasons) and wanted very much to see such a vile place wiped off the world map. So when God changed His mind, the prophet couldn't contain his disgust. He said, in essence, to the Lord, "I *knew* this would happen! Why do You think I ran away from You in the first place, refusing to preach that message to them? I knew very well that You are a compassionate God, and that if these people repented that You would change Your mind too!" (Jonah 4:2).

So we learn that God is immutable and will never, ever change His character. But He can and will change His mind when His people pray. And when we pray, we can remind Him of His unchanging character. He has always been and will always be compassionate. He has always been merciful, He is merciful at this very moment, and He will be that way right into eternity. He will always want to touch people and to answer prayer. He will always be faithful.

We are to make our appeal to God on the basis of His unchanging attributes and His unchanging character.

Partnering with God

In Ezekiel 22:30, we have the startling image of God actually seeking someone to partner with in order to show His compassion. The Message paraphrase captures it like this:

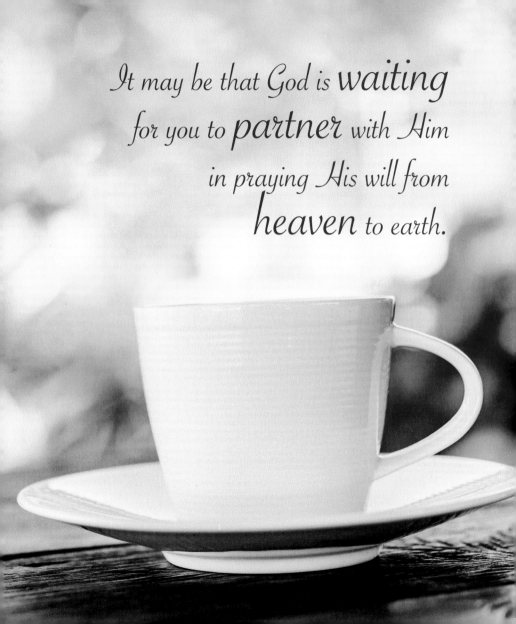

It may be that God is *waiting*
for you to **partner** with Him
in praying His will from
heaven to earth.

I looked for someone to stand up for me against all this, to repair the defenses of the city, to take a stand for me and stand in the gap to protect this land so I wouldn't have to destroy it. I couldn't find anyone. Not one.

God is saying, "I just wanted one person to join hands with Me. I *wanted* to be compassionate and merciful to this people. I *wanted* even one man or woman who would step up and believe for their restoration. But I couldn't find anyone. I looked and looked, and couldn't find one single person who would do this."

What a stunning passage. And it leaves us with a good question to ponder. In what areas of your life does God want you to join hands with Him? In your job? In your future spouse? In your finances? In your family? In your health? What specific men and women in your neighborhood, at your school, or in your carpool does God want you to join hands with Him in moving toward salvation?

It may be that God is waiting for you to partner with Him in praying His will from heaven to earth. He has given you that privilege and ability, and if you pray—consistently and persistently like the widow in Luke 18—He will move. Just as He once gave the stewardship of the earth to Adam (before Adam forfeited it to Satan), so He gives the stewardship of your life to you. He gives the stewardship of your family to you. He gives the stewardship of your finances to you.

Whether you are blessed or not, whether you walk in the principles of God or not, is up to you. God created you in His image, and because God has a will, you have a will. Which means you can choose to cooperate with what God wants to do.

God is looking for a person to do just that—through prayer.

What have you neglected to pray for in your life?

Do you pray when you're in the car?

How much time have you spent praying over your marriage?

How much time have you invested praying over your children?

How much time have you taken to pray over your city? Nation? World?

It's amazing how we want God to be active in our lives and do things for us and through us, but we spend very little time asking Him to do those very things.

God will move when we pray.

Müller was famous for
never doing anything that
wasn't rooted in prayer.

George Müller was one of the greatest pastors and missionaries who ever lived. What many people don't realize is that Müller lived a very sinful life until he was twenty years old. He had been in training for the ministry in his native Germany but continued in his rebellious, ungodly ways. The only reason he was studying to be a pastor was that ministers in that time and place were employees of the state and the ministry was considered a safe, steady job.

In his twentieth year, however, while at Halle University, Müller attended a small-group meeting of some genuine, on-fire believers and gave his life to the Lord. In the days and weeks that followed, he prayed, asking the Lord, "What do You want me to do? Do You still want me to be a minister?"

And God spoke in his heart: *I want you to be a missionary.*

But Müller's father, who was paying for his study, was opposed to the idea. "You need to keep training to be a minister," he said, "so you'll have a regular income."

Müller went back to the Lord and prayed about what course

he should take. After weeks of waiting on God, he had an answer: *Don't depend on your father for support. I will provide for you.*

So Müller stopped taking money from his father, though he had two years of university left and no money for tuition. He prayed for God's provision, and almost immediately he was offered a position teaching German to several visiting American professors. This work made him enough money to finish school.

Müller volunteered for missionary work in several places, but each time his plans fell through. So again he prayed—this time for a full year. Finally the Lord told him, *You have waited long enough. Now go.*

Leaving his native Germany, Müller traveled to London to work with a missionary society there, but then he felt God's leading to travel to another English town. Approaching the door of the only church in the town, he asked to see the pastor.

"Our pastor resigned last week," the church officers told him.

"I've been training as a missionary . . ." Müller began.

"You're hired," they told him.

After a few months, he was dismayed to learn that the

church supported itself principally by renting pews to wealthy members—so they could always be assured of good seats. Müller stopped that practice and refused to take a salary, choosing instead to depend on prayer and free-will offerings.

As a result of his leadership and good teaching, people began to give the way God had instructed, and the offerings increased. The same thing happened when he moved to the town of Bristol to pastor a church there.

Then God put it on Müller's heart to open an orphanage.

As always, Müller spent time praying about this possibility, seeking God's direction. He never mentioned his desire or his needs from the pulpit, and he never sent out any fund-raising letters; he simply prayed. And someone came up to him and said, seemingly out of the blue, "Pastor, I would like to give you the money to start an orphanage."

They did it. They started one orphanage, then another. And over the course of Müller's sixty-plus years as a missionary-pastor, he started more orphanages than any missionary or missions organization since. Müller always emphasized that missions giving should only consist of monies over and above a person's regular tithe. But God proved Himself faithful. In fact, the missions account of his church brought in seven and a half million dollars—and this in the 1800s!

Müller spent the rest of his long and fruitful life leading churches and orphanages, preaching both in England and abroad, and praying! He was famous for never doing anything that wasn't rooted in prayer. One story in particular illustrates both his faithfulness and the amazing power of prayer.

In 1844, when Müller was thirty-nine years old, he committed himself to pray for the conversion of five men he knew. According to his journals, he prayed every day "without a single intermission, whether sick or in health, on land or at sea." And after eighteen months, one of those men accepted Christ.

Müller thanked God and kept praying. Five years later the next man was converted, and six years after that, the third man gave his life to Christ.

Müller kept praying for the final two, but they remained unconverted. When he died at age ninety-three, he had been praying for them more than fifty-two years, seemingly without result. But at his funeral, one of those men said yes to Christ. A short time afterward, the fifth man was converted.

God answers prayer. He does it in His way and in His time, but He responds to the faithful, persistent prayers of His sons and daughters.

What's more, He isn't impatient like the crusty old judge in Jesus' story, and He never gets tired of our coming to Him.

Instead God welcomes us into His presence and leans forward to listen when we pray.

Lord, I pray right now for the one reading these words. The hours and days of life fly by so quickly for all of us. Suddenly it's time for bed, and we realize we've hardly spoken to You all day. We've had small triumphs we haven't shared with You. We've had worries weigh on our hearts and shoulders, and we didn't come to You to unburden. We've had people we deeply care about enduring hard moments on their journey, and we haven't asked You to brighten their path or lighten their load. It's not that we don't believe in prayer. We just get too preoccupied to think about it. Forgive us, Lord. And as Your disciples asked so long ago, "Teach us to pray."

In Jesus' name we pray, amen.

An organization called the Lighthouse of Prayer Movement decided to perform a test on the effectiveness of praying for strangers. The organizers randomly selected two sets of 80 names from a certain city's phone book, and listed them on two separate pages. A group of Christians began to pray, faithfully, every day, for the first group of 80. But no one prayed for the names on the second list. The prayers continued daily for six weeks.

At the end of the six weeks, they called all 160 names they had selected from the phone book, and invited them to church. In the second group of 80, the ones who had not been prayed for, not a single person responded to the invitation. Within the first group, however, sixty-two out of the eighty people on the list said that they would come to church. And they did!

Prayer works—even in the lives of randomly selected strangers! God hears our requests, and if we pray according to His will and His Word, He will answer.

God answers prayer.
He does it in His way
and in His time,

but He responds to the faithful,

persistent prayers of

His sons and daughters.

Chapter 2

Building Bridges to Heaven

*I*ntercession probably isn't a word you use every day. Or maybe you've never used it at all. It has a heavy sound to it and doesn't seem like anything that would be a warm, happy, familiar, or helpful part of our lives.

But it can become all of those things—and a great deal more.

An incredible truth about God and our prayers to Him resides within that single word. It's actually speaking about a bridge—a bridge that leads toward authentic joy in your prayer life.

It's also a bridge with the potential to change your world.

Jesus Intercedes for Us

In Romans 8:33–34 we read:

> Who shall bring a charge against God's elect? It is God who
> justifies. Who is he who condemns? It is Christ who died,
> and furthermore is also risen, who is even at the right hand
> of God, who also makes intercession for us.

Where is Jesus Christ today? The Bible leaves no doubt:
He is at the right hand of God the Father, making intercession
for us.

Now look a little further into the New Testament at Hebrews
7:24–25:

> But [Jesus], because He continues forever, has an unchange-
> able priesthood. Therefore He is also able to save to the
> uttermost those who come to God through Him, since He
> always lives to make intercession for them.

Twice, then, we see that Jesus makes intercession for us. In fact, He "always lives" to make this intercession. That's encouraging . . . as far as we understand it. But what does it really mean? What *is* intercession, anyway?

I want to make a point here that may shock you a little: Intercession is not a prayer. Why do I say that? Because intercession is an activity. It's an *action*. At the same time, however, you can say a prayer of intercession.

We could say the same thing about faith. Faith is not a prayer. Faith is an action. But you can offer a prayer of faith. The apostle James says very clearly that if your faith is not active—if it isn't working—then it's not really faith at all. It's dead.

But back to intercession. If it's an action, what kind of action is it?

Intercession is the act of bringing two parties together. It's bridging a gap, making a connection that couldn't otherwise be made.

This is an action that Jesus performed and continues to perform on our behalf. He brings us together with the Father. In

Intercession is a
bridge that leads
toward authentic joy
in your prayer life.
It's also a bridge
with the potential to
change your world.

the gospel of John, Jesus said, "In My Father's house are many mansions; if it were not so, I would have told you. I go to prepare a place for you" (14:2–3). And then He told them plainly, "No one comes to the Father except through Me" (v. 6).

In other words, "I'm about to take an action that will enable you to dwell with the Father in heaven. You can't dwell with Him now. You can't have a relationship with a holy God unless I build a bridge—unless I perform the ultimate act of intercession."

We have an English word that sounds similar to "*intercession*," and it's a good simile for the word.

Intersection.

What is an intersection? It's where two roads meet or come together. We speak about the intersection of First Street and Mulberry Lane.

What makes intercession an action word here? *Jesus brings our way into an intersection with God's way.* That's what He did for us and still does for us. We couldn't reach to God; we couldn't intersect with God's way on our own. Our paths would never cross in a billion years. But Jesus built a bridge for us by laying down His life. In Colossians, the apostle Paul puts it this way:

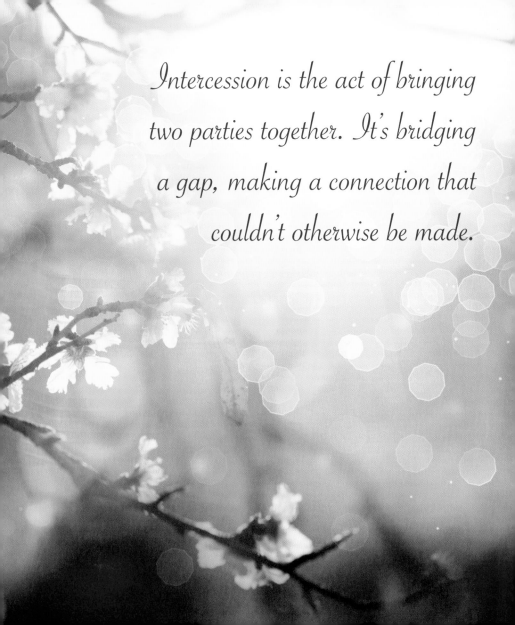

Intercession is the act of bringing two parties together. It's bridging a gap, making a connection that couldn't otherwise be made.

And you, who once were alienated and enemies in your mind by wicked works, yet now He has reconciled in the body of His flesh through death, to present you holy, and blameless, and above reproach in His sight. (1:21–22)

Jesus became the bridge—the bridge over troubled waters—allowing us to draw near to God, and we couldn't have gotten there any other way.

Fulfilling the prophecy of Isaiah (53:12), Jesus "poured out His soul unto death," dying on a cross. He was "numbered with the transgressors," with two thieves crucified on His right and on His left. He carried "the sin of many" and made "intercession for the transgressors"—that's you and me. In so doing, He made a bridge for sinful people like us to be able to cross over a huge divide, a great chasm, and enter into a relationship with a holy God.

Picture the Grand Canyon, but a thousand times wider and a thousand times deeper. Jesus Himself became the bridge over that nameless and terrible depth, allowing us to enter into the very throne room of God Almighty and approach Him with confidence.

The Holy Spirit Intercedes for Us

Let's look back now at Romans 8:

> Likewise the Spirit also helps in our weaknesses. For we do
> not know what we should pray for as we ought, but the Spirit
> Himself makes intercession for us with groanings which
> cannot be uttered. Now He who searches the hearts knows
> what the mind of the Spirit is, because He makes interces-
> sion for the saints according to the will of God. (vv. 26–27)

What is this passage saying? It's telling us that often we
don't know how or for what we should pray. We don't know how
to pray for God's will in a specific circumstance. We don't know
what the mind of God might be concerning life situations that
cause us anxiety or perplexity or weigh on our hearts. We just
don't know.

But the Holy Spirit knows.

So the Spirit Himself makes intercession for us. He creates
a bridge for us "with groanings which cannot be uttered."

We might find ourselves confused about the will of God in a given circumstance, but the Spirit isn't confused at all. He knows God's will perfectly. So when we pray, the Holy Spirit helps to make an intersection or bridge between our will and God's will, allowing us to pray according to the will of God.

The Romans 8 passage says, "The Spirit also helps in our weaknesses." The Greek term translated "helps" refers to a situation where two parties mutually bear a burden. If you and I were carrying a heavy couch into a moving van, you might take the front end and I would take the back end, and we would move it together. I wouldn't be strong enough to pick up that couch and carry it myself, but if you take the other end, we can manage it together.

That's what the Holy Spirit does for us in our prayers. He comes alongside us to help. He says, "Here I am. Let Me help you lift that. Let's carry that into the Father's presence together! You pick it up, and I'll pick it up with you." The Spirit wants to help you carry your burdens to God.

"Carry your burdens to God"—that's what prayer really is! A very simple definition of prayer is *the transference of a burden.* Prayer is when we have a burden or weight on our heart—about our health, our family, our business, or one of our children— and we go to God and give Him that burden.

David wrote,

> *Cast your burden on the LORD,*
> *And He shall sustain you. (Psalm 55:22)*

The apostle Peter added, "Cast all your anxiety on him because he cares for you" (1 Peter 5:7 NIV).

That's what we do in prayer, and we ought to do it again and again in the course of our days. We cast our cares and anxieties and worries and concerns on Him, knowing that He loves us, cares for us, and will sustain us. He's the one who makes it possible for us to carry the burden. In fact, He's the one who does all the heavy lifting.

If you find yourself burdened and weighed down about *any-thing* as you read these words, set down the book for a while,

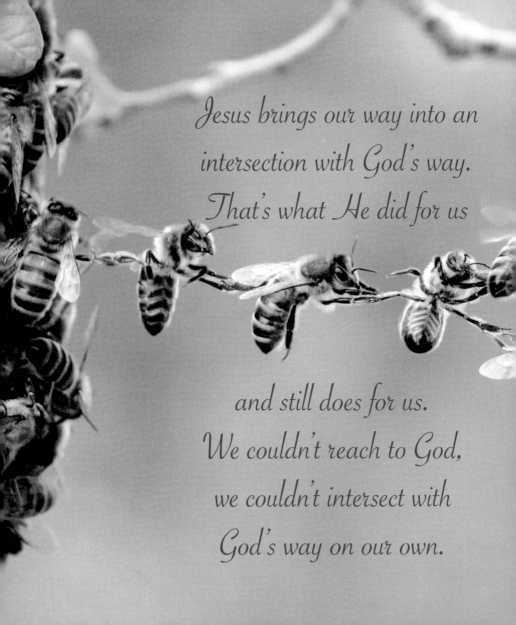

Jesus brings our way into an intersection with God's way. That's what He did for us and still does for us. We couldn't reach to God, we couldn't intersect with God's way on our own.

Prayer is when we have a burden or weight
on our heart——about our health, our family,
our business, or one of our children——and
we go to God and give Him that burden.

go to God, and give Him your burden. And leave it there with Him—don't be tempted to pick it up again.

Have you ever taken a bundle of clothes to the dry cleaners and then, without thinking, scooped them up from the counter and walked halfway back to your car with them? (Maybe it's just me!) Taking those dirty clothes back to the car and driving around with them won't do you or the garments any good. There's no sense making a trip to the cleaners if you don't leave the dirty clothes on the counter.

In the same way, if you come away from your prayer time with your shoulders just as weighed down as when you began to pray, then you didn't pray at all. You just griped!

Have you ever done any backpacking on wilderness trails? If you have, you know that pack can get really heavy. You have to carry everything you'll need with you—a tent, a sleeping bag, food, cooking gear, and water. Some of those packs can weigh up to forty or fifty pounds.

But when you've hiked several miles, maybe even uphill, you will eventually come to a place where you take a break, get a drink of water, and relax for a while. And nothing compares to that feeling of slipping your arms and shoulders out from under that heavy pack and setting it down on the ground. You suddenly feel so light you think you could fly.

That's what the Holy Spirit wants to do for you. He wants to help you slip that heavy weight off your shoulders and leave it before your Father's throne. He's ready and waiting to help you carry that burden. And as you call out to Him more and more, He will become much more than a burden bearer to you. He will become your best Friend.

When you are praying with the help of the Holy Spirit, however, you may hear yourself saying some things you weren't even thinking about when you began to pray. Let's look at the Romans 8 passage again in The Message paraphrase:

Meanwhile, the moment we get tired in the waiting, God's Spirit is right alongside helping us along. If we don't know how or what to pray, it doesn't matter. He does our praying in and for us, making prayer out of our wordless sighs, our aching groans. He knows us far better than we know ourselves. (vv. 26–27)

In the same way, if you come away from your prayer time with your shoulders just as weighed down as when you began to pray, then you didn't pray at all. You just griped!

Did you get that? He prays *in* us and *for* us.

After church not long ago, a couple came up to me at the front of the auditorium with a prayer request. "Hey, Pastor Robert, we're talking about making an offer on a house that's nearer to the church. We don't live very close, and it's a long drive every Sunday. Besides that, the new house is in a better school system. We're excited about it. Would you pray for us to be able to buy this house?"

I said I would be happy to do that and, putting a hand on each of their shoulders, I began to pray. As I began to speak to the Lord out loud, however, I found myself praying in a way I hadn't intended. I heard myself saying, "Lord, if this house *isn't* Your will for them, if this *isn't* the best house, if this *isn't* the one You have picked out for them, I pray they will find out some things they don't know about it. I pray they will lose their peace and pull out."

That wasn't what I had expected to pray at all, and I felt a little bit awkward because I'm sure it wasn't what *they* had been expecting either.

The next week I saw them again and asked, "What happened on the house?"

The husband said, "Well, we found out some things that we didn't know about. We lost our peace and pulled out." His report to me was almost word for word what I had prayed for them the week before. In fact, they ended up finding another house that was even better.

That's how the Holy Spirit intercedes for us—by praying in us and for us.

But you might also say that the Holy Spirit *intervenes* for us on our behalf. He steps in because we don't always have a handle on the will of God, and we don't know what to pray for or how we ought to pray.

So Jesus intercedes for us, and the Holy Spirit intercedes for us.

But there is one more important piece to the puzzle.

We Intercede for Others

Scripture tells us that when we say prayers of intercession, we are building bridges between God and the people for whom we pray.

As you *call out*
to God **more** and **more**,
He will **become** much more
than a burden **bearer** to you.
He will **become** your
best *Friend.*

Remember, this isn't just a prayer, it's a deliberate action. It isn't just saying words, it's a construction project. In 1 Timothy 2:1–2, Paul writes:

> Therefore I exhort first of all that supplications, prayers, intercessions, and giving of thanks be made for all men, for kings and all who are in authority, that we may lead a quiet and peaceable life in all godliness and reverence.

Because Jesus has done the work of intercession and still intercedes for us with the Father, and because the Holy Spirit intercedes for us as well, helping us unburden ourselves, we can now intercede for others. The Lord Jesus and the Holy Spirit have built bridges to God that we may cross over, so that we, too, can be in that bridge-building business. We have the incredible privilege of building a span from heaven to earth, from God to the person for whom we are praying.

Let's imagine you have a twenty-year-old son named Josh who hasn't been walking with the Lord. You're concerned that he's being drawn into the wrong crowd and straying into some dark areas, and you want to intercede for him.

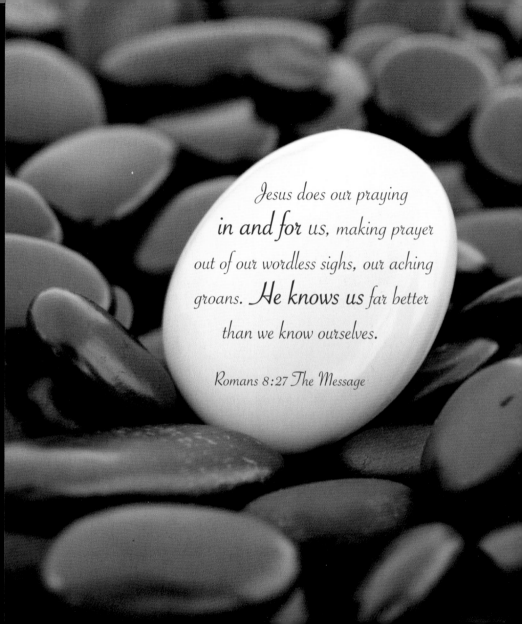

Jesus does our praying
in and for us, making prayer
out of our wordless sighs, our aching
groans. *He knows us* far better
than we know ourselves.

Romans 8:27 The Message

So you come to God with this crushing weight on your heart because you love Josh, because you're deeply concerned for him and some of the choices he's been making, because you feel helpless to change his course. What do you do? How do you intercede for him?

First, you take hold of God.

When the disciples came to Jesus and asked Him how to pray, He told them, essentially, "The first thing you do is to honor God. You say,

> *Our Father in heaven,*
> *Hallowed be Your name. (Matthew 6:9)*

Your version might be something like this: "Father, I thank You that You made a bridge for me. I thank You for saving me by grace through faith, through the Lord Jesus Christ. I thank You, God, that You are an all-knowing, all-powerful God. You are a loving God and a merciful God, and I praise You for Your greatness . . . for Your wisdom . . . for Your kindness to me . . ."

You take hold of God by acknowledging who He is and by thanking Him and praising Him for all He has done.

Second, you take hold of Josh.

You say, "Lord, You know the weight on my heart today. I'm bringing Josh to You right now. I ask You to protect him. I ask You, dear Father, to take away all the evil influences of friends around him who are trying to lead him in a wrong direction. I ask You, Lord, even to replace those friends with other friends who know You and love You and will bring Josh to You. You know this deep concern on my heart, Lord, I can't hide it from You. So I bring it to You, in Jesus' name."

Do you see how that works?

You take hold of God in one hand and take hold of Josh in the other hand, and you become a bridge in between them. You stand in the gap for your son. You pray, "God, I'm bringing Josh to You, and I'm asking for a miracle in his life. I'm asking that the Holy Spirit will go to Josh and convict him of the way he has been living. I know that this is Your will, Father, and that right now I am praying in Your will."

So you pray for Josh, and don't give up on him, no matter what. You *continue* to pray until there is an intersection between

Scripture tells us that when we say prayers of intercession, we are building bridges between God and the people for whom we pray.

Josh and God, until Josh finally runs into God's arms and God's way becomes his way.

Jesus Himself said it: "Pray always, and don't give up."

Remember the woman who prayed for her unsaved husband? Day after day, week after week, year after year, and decade after decade, she took God in one hand and her husband in the other. And eventually, *after forty-two years*, she made an intersection for her husband to run into God.

Remember George Müller praying for his unsaved friend every day, even on his deathbed? It took more than fifty years, but Müller prayed faithfully until the connection was made.

The reason they could do that—the reason any of us can do this—is because Jesus has first made a bridge for us and an intersection for us.

You and I can't begin to imagine what that cost Him.

Not long ago I read a story in a history book. After World War I, the United States government allocated funds to help care for the orphans in Europe. At one of the orphanages, an emaciated man brought in a very thin little girl. He said, "I would like for you to take care of my little girl, please."

They asked him if the girl was his daughter, and he said yes. "We're so sorry," they told him, "but our rules and policies are such that we can't take in any children who have a living parent."

"But I was in prison camps during the war," he protested. "And now I'm too sick to work. Her mother's gone. She will die if you don't take care of her!"

The officials felt compassion for the distressed man but told him their hands were tied. There was nothing they could do.

Finally the man said, "Do you mean to tell me that if I were dead, you would take care of my little girl, and she could have food and clothes and a home?"

"Yes," they replied.

With that, the man picked up the little girl, hugged her and kissed her, and then put her hand in the hand of the man at the desk. "I will arrange it," he said. He walked out of the orphanage and sacrificed his own life.

Why do I tell that story?

You take hold of God in one hand and
take hold of a person in the other hand,
and you become a bridge in between them.

Only because it reminds me of another story.

Somewhere in eternity, the day came when Jesus said to the Father, "Do You mean that if I die, those people on earth can live and have a home with You forever?"

And the Father said, "Yes."

With that, Jesus put our hands in the Father's hand, walked out of heaven, was born on earth, and died on the cross and paid for our sins. In so doing, He made a bridge for us so that we could have a relationship with a holy God.

If you have never done so, you need to walk across the bridge that Jesus provided for you at the cost of His own blood, His own life.

Then, remembering that Jesus built that bridge for you (and with the Spirit's help), you can begin to intercede for others, so that their paths will intersect with the path of God and they will walk with Him forever.

Lord, thank You for building a bridge for us. We know all too well that we could have never crossed over into Life, into a relationship with God—not in a million years—if You hadn't made a way for us. Thank You for Your Holy Spirit, who takes the heavy load of worries and fears off of our shoulders and carries our burdens. Now, Lord, help us to build bridges for others. Help us to pray and not give up. Help us to hold on to You with one hand and on to our loved ones and friends with the other until their way becomes Your way.

In Jesus' name we pray, amen.

I've been getting my hair cut at the same place for at least twenty years. A few years ago, I was in the chair for my haircut and overheard a lady in the chair next to me talking to her hairdresser. She was pouring out her heart, as women often do with other women, telling the hairdresser about her miscarriages and how deeply she and her husband wanted a child. She hadn't married until she was thirty-five, and they had wanted a baby as soon as possible. But now she had experienced three heartbreaking miscarriages.

As the stylist finished my hair cut, the Lord spoke to me prompting me to pray for this woman. As it turned out, she was getting up at the same time, and as we both walked toward the cashier, I spoke to her.

"Ma'am," I said, "I know you don't know me. I'm a pastor here in the area, and I couldn't help hearing your conversation just now. I feel like the Lord spoke to me, and wants me to pray for you. But I'm also supposed to tell you something."

I looked her right in the eyes and said, "God is going to give you a child."

Immediately, the woman began to weep. I repeated, "God is going to give you a child, but He is arranging some things in your life right now. Would you mind if I prayed for you?"

"No," she said, tears streaming down her face. "Please do."

And I prayed for her right there in front of the cash register.

Not long after this, she and her husband, who had not been churchgoers, began attending our church. A few weeks later, she came down to the front of the auditorium after the service, where our prayer team was praying for people, and I had the opportunity to pray for her again. "I've given control of my life to God," she told me afterward, "and released my bitterness toward Him."

They became members of our church, and, in God's timing, He gave the couple a beautiful little girl.

I had never intended to eavesdrop on this woman's heartbroken conversation at the hair salon, but God had placed me in the right chair at the right time and prompted me to pray. When we are sensitive to God's Spirit leading us to pray for others, and we follow through, He will come through in ways we can't imagine.

Jesus put our hands in the Father's hand,
walked out of heaven, was born on earth,
and died on the cross and paid for our sins.
In so doing, He made a bridge for us so that
we could have a relationship with a holy God.

Chapter 3

Keeping the Prayer Line Open

Do you remember why Jesus told His disciples the story of the persistent widow and the judge? Luke says he did it "to illustrate their need for constant prayer and to show them that they must keep praying until the answer comes" (Luke 18:1 TLB).

The Lord Himself was saying we need to pray very often—or almost all the time. Constantly. So why don't we? If we've been given the greatest privilege in the universe, a wide-open door to come before the Creator and the King of kings with every detail and concern of our lives, what's holding us back?

I think I know at least part of that answer. We often neglect to pray because we become discouraged and defeated over our failures and sins.

The author of Hebrews 12 levels a strong warning about this right in the middle of his encouragement to run a great race in life:

> Therefore we also, since we are surrounded by so great a cloud of witnesses, let us lay aside every weight, and the sin which so easily ensnares us, and let us run with endurance the race that is set before us. (v. 1)

Our whole life, be it long or short, is a race that we are called to run well—run to win, serving the Lord. But the only way we'll be able to accomplish this, the writer tells us, is to "lay aside . . . the sin which so easily ensnares us." The New Living Translation translates that phrase as, "the sin that so easily trips us up."

Do you have a sin that easily ensnares you? Do you have a sin in your life that continually trips you up and causes you to stumble?

More to the point, do you have a sin that holds you back from the practice of constant prayer?

What We Do Instead

I have a friend who is a believer, who loves the Lord dearly, and yet is hooked on cigarettes. He has tried for years and years to quit. He once said to me, "If I stop smoking, Pastor, you and my wife won't have anything to talk about—because I'll be perfect."

And that's the way many of us feel about those ensnaring bad habits and sins.

But God offers us a remedy for our most devastating, persistent sins. The trouble is, too often we fail to embrace that remedy. Here are some of the things we tend to do instead.

We Doubt Our Salvation

When you find yourself repeating the same sin over and over again, do you ever ask yourself, "Am I really saved at all? Do I really have a relationship with Christ? How could I do this if I belong to Him?"

I remember a sin in my life that I struggled with for years and years. I can recall my very thoughts: *I wish I could just start over and get saved again. And then I could say, "All of this struggle was* before *I received the Lord.*" But I couldn't really say that, because I've had to deal with a good bit of junk and garbage in my life *since* my salvation in Christ. And I'm guessing you are dealing with some of that refuse from your old life as well.

Have you ever imagined God kicking you out of the family? I have.

I've imagined Him saying to me, "Okay, fella, that was the last straw. You've done this too many times. I've forgiven you time after time, but now I've just had it. Pack your bags."

I've had the mental picture of God opening the door and some burly angel pushing me out into the cold. And while God is still closing the door, in my mind I can hear Him turning to other members of the family and saying, "Who let that guy in? What was I thinking allowing Robert Morris into the family? It's been—what—twenty years, and he *still* hasn't overcome this sin?"

Can you relate to that terrible mental picture? I think a lot of us can.

Thank goodness that will never happen—because God is faithful and will never leave us or forsake us and because salvation is by grace. *Whew!*

God offers us a remedy for
our most devastating, persistent sins.
The trouble is that we too often
fail to embrace that remedy.

The trouble is, we can lose sight of that truth. And when we do, chances are we'll neglect to pray.

We Berate and Beat Up on Ourselves

Even if we don't actually doubt our salvation, we can still do a number on ourselves on account of our stubborn sins. We often give our "inner man" a good chewing out—and engage in some serious character assassination.

You are such a jerk. An idiot. You are a dirtbag. You are pond scum.

In some parts of the world, misguided Christians actually flog themselves with whips during Holy Week, leaving their backs bleeding and scarred. But we're too sophisticated for that. We simply flog ourselves with cynical, cutting thoughts and words.

We Make Wild Resolutions

Here's something else we might do in response to our sins. "O, God," we say, "if You will forgive me, I will *never* do that again. You need to understand how bad I feel about what I have done. From now on, I will be on my guard, and I will be a different person."

The bottom line of all these techniques we use on ourselves, however, is that they simply don't work. (I know this, because I've tried them all.) Making wild promises and resolutions and putting ourselves under more law only compounds the guilt.

There is only one way to deal with sin in your life, and it is God's way.

God's Remedy for Sin

God Himself called David "a man after My own heart" (Acts 13:22).

That was written about David in the New Testament, hundreds of years after he reigned as king in Israel. It was also recorded in Scripture *after* he had committed adultery, deception, and murder. Think about that!

Obviously, David learned to handle his sin God's way—in a way that brought him closer to God instead of keeping him away. In Psalm 51, David's brokenhearted psalm of confession, we see four secrets for how to approach God with our sins.

God is faithful and will never
leave us or forsake us and
because salvation is by grace.

Secret Number One: Admit

> *Have mercy upon me, O God,*
> *According to Your lovingkindness;*
> *According to the multitude of Your tender mercies,*
> *Blot out my transgressions.*
> *Wash me thoroughly from my iniquity,*
> *And cleanse me from my sin.*
> *For I acknowledge my transgressions,*
> *And my sin is always before me. (Psalm 51:1–3)*

Notice the words *me* and *my* in the first three verses.

- "Have mercy upon *me* . . ."
- "Blot out *my* transgressions."
- "Wash *me* thoroughly from *my* iniquity . . ."
- "Cleanse *me* from *my* sin"
- "For I acknowledge *my* transgressions . . ."
- "*My* sin is always before *me*."

David isn't being egotistical with all these *me* statements. He's just being brutally honest about who's responsible for his sin. He's saying, "Lord, I make no attempt to justify, whitewash, or hide the ugliness of this sin. I acknowledge it before You. I admit it."

This is the first step to overcoming sin: admit it. Confess. Stop sweeping sin under the carpet and pretending that it isn't there.

Simple, right? Not necessarily. When you and I are dealing with a sin that has tripped us up again and again, we may come to a place where we stop confessing it at all.

Why do we do that? Because we imagine that God must be weary of hearing it. We think to ourselves, *God has heard me say this so many times it must thoroughly disgust Him. I can't go back to Him with this again.* And that is precisely what our enemy encourages us to think. He whispers, *Quit telling this to God.*

But what happens when you stop confessing a particular thought or action as sin? Before long, you will stop considering it as sin. You will begin to think of it as a normal-though-regrettable part of life, something you will "just have to live with."

There is only
one way
to deal with
sin in your life,
and it is
God's way.

So you live with it. As a result, you must also live apart from the presence and power of the Holy Spirit in your life.

Here is a verse you might know very well but may possibly need to consider once again:

> If we confess our sins, He is faithful and just to forgive us our sins and to cleanse us from all unrighteousness. (1 John 1:9)

This is God's remedy for dealing with sin. And I want you to notice something very important about this verse. It begins with the word *if*.

If we confess our sins . . . He will forgive and cleanse us.

But *if* we get tired of coming to God with the same sin over and over again, *if* we tell ourselves that God is sick of our even approaching Him, then we get discouraged and give up. We don't confess our sins, and then we lose out on experiencing the great joy and freedom of His forgiveness and the power of the Holy Spirit filling our lives afresh. Beyond that, we end up attempting to serve God with an impure conscience. We find ourselves trying to earn God's love and forgiveness instead of simply living in it.

This is the first step to overcoming sin: *admit it.* *Confess.* Stop sweeping sin under the carpet and pretending that it isn't there.

So you must confess your sins—acknowledging them and agreeing with God about them—if you want to move forward with joy and freedom in your Christian life.

Let me give you a little background on the familiar verse we've just looked at in 1 John 1:9. The letters, or epistles, that we call 1 John, 2 John, and 3 John were the last New Testament books to be written. First John was written by the apostle John to the church at Ephesus near the end of the first century. He wrote the letter specifically to combat the twisted theology of a group called the Gnostics, who were gaining ascendance at that time and had infiltrated the church at Ephesus.

The word *Gnostic* comes from the Greek word *ginosko*, which means "to know." And that's what mattered to the Gnostics—"knowledge" as they defined it. The Gnostics were like many of today's modern-day cults that claim extrabiblical revelation. They boasted of understanding that the rest of the church didn't have, and further claimed that an angel—not the Holy Spirit—had given them these insights. And they taught that if you really wanted to be on the inside track in the Christian life, you had to possess this so-called knowledge.

That's why John begins his letter by saying, "This is the message which we have heard from Him and declare to you . . ." (1 John 1:5). In other words, "I didn't come by these words from some angel or mysterious messenger. I heard them directly from Jesus Himself, so listen up."

It is in that context that John goes on to proclaim the real truth about sin, self-deception, and how we find forgiveness:

> If we claim that we're free of sin, we're only fooling ourselves. . . . On the other hand, if we admit our sins—make a clean breast of them—he won't let us down; he'll be true to himself. He'll forgive our sins and purge us of all wrongdoing. If we claim that we've never sinned, we out-and-out contradict God—make a liar out of him. A claim like that only shows off our ignorance of God. I write this, dear children, to guide you out of sin. But if anyone does sin, we have [an Advocate] in the presence of the Father: Jesus Christ, righteous Jesus. When he served as a sacrifice for our sins, he solved the sin problem for good—not only ours, but the whole world's. (1 John 1:8–2:2 MSG)

You must confess your sins——
acknowledging them and agreeing
with God about them——if you
want to move forward with joy
and freedom in your Christian life.

He's basically saying that if you claim you don't have any sin, you're a liar, and the truth isn't in you! But when you do sin, remember that you have an Advocate with the Father, who is Jesus Christ the Lord. Confess that sin to the Father in Jesus' name, and you will be forgiven.

If then, you are ever going to overcome an ensnaring sin, a sin that continually trips you up, there's only one place to start. You must come clean with God and yourself about your sin: Admit it. And when you've done that, you must agree it's wrong.

Secret Number Two: Agree

> *Against You, You only, have I sinned,*
> *And done this evil in Your sight—*
> *That You may be found just when You speak,*
> *And blameless when You judge. (Psalm 51:4)*

David begins his heartfelt prayer of confession by saying, in effect, "I *admit* that I did certain things." Then he continues by saying, "I *agree* those things were sinful." If we ever stop doing these two things—admitting our sin and agreeing that it is wrong in God's sight—we will remain in bondage to our sin.

In other words, we need to stop justifying ourselves and making excuses for our sin and instead accept responsibility for our actions.

Not long ago I heard about a woman who got drunk on New Year's Eve. One of her friends said to her the next day, "I heard that you had a little too much to drink last night."

"Yes," the woman replied, "and I just hate it when I get overserved. I told them not to serve me so much, but they did it anyway, so I got drunk."

Overserved? That's not owning the sin. That's not agreeing with God that it was wrong. We may be tempted to laugh at this woman or judge her for her attempt at evasion. But don't we all evade the truth about our actions at one time or another?

"Yes, I guess I lost my cool. But if you'd had the day I had . . ."

Or "if you had the boss I have . . ."

Or "if you had the husband (or wife) I have . . ."

Or "if you had the migraine I had . . ."

Or "if you were under the stress I've been under . . ."

If . . . you are ever going to

overcome an ensnaring sin,

a sin that continually trips you up,

there's only one place to start.

You must come clean with

God and yourself . . .

If you want to experience God's forgiveness and escape the tentacles of an ensnaring sin, you have to stop justifying what you have said or done. You need to say to your Father, "You are right, God. What I did in that moment was plain old sin. I agree with You that it was wrong." And once you've done that, you can move on to the next step.

Secret Number Three: Ask

> *Create in me a clean heart, O God,*
> *And renew a steadfast spirit within me. . . .*
> *Restore to me the joy of Your salvation,*
> *And uphold me by Your generous Spirit. (Psalm 51:10, 12)*

The essence of what David is saying here is, *"I ask You* to create in me a clean heart. *I ask You* to renew a steadfast or right spirit within me. *I ask You* to restore my joy and uphold me by Your Spirit."

Psalm 51 was written right after the prophet Nathan confronted David about his hidden sins. All of us have experienced shame from sin in our lives, but how much guilt and shame would you feel if you had done what David did: commit adultery and murder?

Psalm 32, also penned by David after his sinful acts, spells out the agonizing effects in great detail but also shares how he found relief:

> *When I refused to confess my sin,*
> *my body wasted away,*
> *and I groaned all day long.*
> *Day and night your hand of discipline was heavy on me.*
> *My strength evaporated like water in the summer heat.*
> *Finally, I confessed all my sins to you*
> *and stopped trying to hide my guilt.*
> *I said to myself, "I will confess my rebellion to the LORD."*
> *And you forgave me! All my guilt is gone. (vv. 3–5 NLT)*

That last verse reveals the simple but wonderful truth: God forgives us when we ask. But we have to ask!

In the case of a sin that keeps coming back into our lives, a

If you want to
experience God's forgiveness and escape
the tentacles of an ensnaring sin, you have to
stop justifying what you have said or done.

sin we feel we will never overcome, the problem is usually that we've stopped asking forgiveness. And when we stop *asking*, we stop *receiving*. It's not that God stops giving. It's that we are no longer open to take for ourselves what He has to freely give. After repeatedly refusing to confess a particular sin and ask forgiveness, we begin to have a seared conscience, where we tell ourselves that the sin really isn't a problem.

Again, this has been part of my own story. I've had an ensnaring sin in my life that I got so tired of fighting and so tired of confessing to the Lord—assuming that He was tired of hearing about it—that I would go months at a time without confessing it and would, thus, find myself slipping farther and farther away from the Lord's presence.

That's what David is describing in Psalm 32. When he hid his sin and refused to confess it, he went down both physically and spiritually. Everything about him declined as long as he refused to admit his sin and agree with God about it and ask forgiveness. But when he did finally confess, God forgave him, and all was well.

Don't stop asking for forgiveness from God.

Jesus has already paid for that forgiveness on the cross with His own blood. You just have to ask for it . . . and then accept it.

Secret Number Four: Accept

> *For You do not desire sacrifice, or else I would give it;*
> *You do not delight in burnt offering.*
> *The sacrifices of God are a broken spirit,*
> *A broken and a contrite heart—*
> *These, O God, You will not despise. (Psalm 51:16–17)*

David is saying here, "Listen, God, if You wanted me to go slaughter an animal, I would do it. If that would help, it's just what I'd do. But that's not what You want, is it? What You want is for my heart to be broken over this sin. You want me to admit what I have done and not to hide it anymore. You want me to agree with You, God, that what I've done is wrong. And You want me to ask for Your forgiveness. I've done those things now, dear Lord, so now I'm going to open my arms and accept Your mercy and grace."

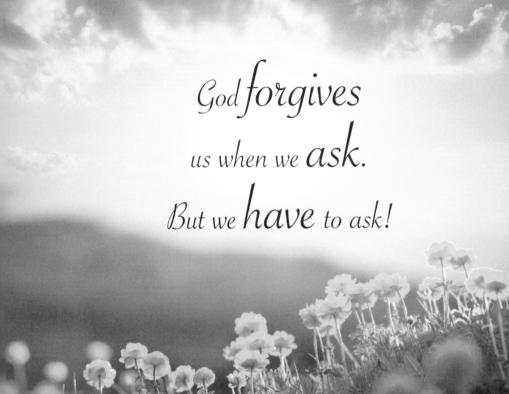

God *forgives*

us when we **ask.**

But we **have** to ask!

He doesn't

want you to

beat yourself up

about your failure.

God doesn't want you to do penance. He doesn't want you to beat yourself up about your failure. He doesn't want you to doubt your salvation. He doesn't want you to put yourself under the burden of more vows or more laws or more rash promises. He simply wants you to accept His remedy for sin and let him cleanse You from all unrighteousness.

The apostle James tells us, "Confess your trespasses to one another, and pray for one another, that you may be healed. The effective, fervent prayer of a righteous man avails much" (James 5:16).

This is God's way. But we struggle with it sometimes.

You would think that after admitting our sin, agreeing with God about our sin, and asking forgiveness for our sin, that we would find it easy to simply accept His forgiveness.

But it's not always easy—or maybe it feels *too* easy.

We imagine that we ought to continue feeling bad, feeling low, feeling defeated for a while, even after we have been forgiven. We think to ourselves that it will help God to know how bad we feel if we walk around with no joy for a while. We imagine that remaining unhappy and miserable will prove we're serious and somehow gain us extra credit with God.

But we don't need extra credit.

We don't need extra grace, extra mercy, extra favor, extra anything to deal with even our most persistent, entangling sins.

What Jesus has already paid is all we will ever need. As Paul said in Romans,

> So, what do you think? With God on our side like this, how can we lose? If God didn't hesitate to put everything on the line for us, embracing our condition and exposing himself to the worst by sending his own Son, is there anything else he wouldn't gladly and freely do for us? (Romans 8:31–32 MSG)

Our part is simply to keep the prayer line open by availing ourselves of the remedy for our ongoing sin.

When we mess up, admit it.

Agree with God that it's wrong.

Ask for forgiveness.

Then open our arms and hearts to accept what He freely and graciously gives.

Open your arms and heart
to accept what *He* freely
and graciously gives.

Father, melt away the stubborn pride that keeps us from admitting our sins and accepting Your cleansing. Forgive us for hanging onto shame that Your Son has already carried for us on His cross. Free us from the foolish notion that we have to punish ourselves or surrender our joy when we have failed You and failed ourselves. Help us to fully embrace the priceless gift of a clean heart and the righteousness of Jesus Himself applied to our account. In other words, Lord, we want to live in freedom and with a light heart. We praise You for making that possible.

In Jesus' name we pray, amen.

I awoke in pain. What happened to me? Immediately the pieces fell into place. I was in the recovery room. My chest had been cracked open, my aortic aneurism repaired and my aortic valve replaced. The caregivers were frantic. Not thinking I would remember a thing, they talked freely. I was in cardiogenic shock and not responding to doses of medicines reserved for last-ditch efforts.

I was dying. As a doctor myself, I knew that very well.

Something told me I had about thirty seconds before I lost consciousness again. All I could think to do was pray. In the few seconds—and not much more—before the room faded once again, I called out to God, *Lord, I don't mind dying. I will be with You. But please let me live one day longer than Laura. She already lost one husband and I don't want her to go through that pain again. And there are a lot of people praying for me. I don't want to let them down.*

Each time I closed my eyes in recovery, I repeated the prayer, not knowing if I would ever open my eyes in this world again. But even with the sickness from the medicine waking me up every fifteen minutes, I was at peace. And with each return of consciousness I was surprised to still be alive. And I kept praying.

This went on for fourteen hours before my vital signs finally stabilized. By the second day, I was out of bed and walked two hundred feet—I felt like I'd just run a marathon. By the fourth day, I was up to 1,700 feet, and the doctor sent me home. My nurse cried as I gathered my things and left the room. She didn't think I would live past day one.

Sometime later, my wife told me that before my surgery, she'd had a vision while she was praying. She had seen Jesus and angels in the operating room.

I also heard that a lot of people were praying for me, but it wasn't until I went home that I found out how massive the prayers were. Churches in Lafayette and Baton Rouge, Louisiana, and even people in Honduras were praying for me. Friends who are Messianic Jews in Israel were praying. The mother of a friend woke up at 4 a.m. and prayed until she went to bed the night of my surgery. She lives in

Juarez, Mexico, and I have never even met her, but I am so thankful for her. A friend in Colombia e-mailed me that he was praying for me. Many friends in Southlake, Texas, and the surrounding area, and members of my church were faithful to pray for me.

When they're sharing the gospel with other people, there's a question that Christians sometimes ask. *If you were to die today, do you know for certain that you would go to heaven?* It's one thing to answer yes to that question in a time of comfort, routine, and safety. But now I had been to the ragged edge of life itself, when my very existence on earth could be measured in single heartbeats.

My answer was yes as I felt the prayers and peace of that certainty around me that day in the recovery room.

Greg Byrne, M.D.

We don't need extra grace,
extra mercy, extra favor, extra anything

to deal with even our most persistent,
entangling sins. What Jesus has
already paid is all we will ever need.

Chapter 4

Receiving and Releasing His Power

I heard about a little boy who went to his dad and said, "I want a little brother."

His dad looked up from his newspaper. "Well, son," he said, "maybe you ought to pray about that."

So the little guy prayed every night for one month. And nothing happened. He went on praying for two months. Still nothing. He continued to pray for three months, but no brother came, so he finally just quit praying.

Some six months after that, the little boy's dad took him to the hospital, pulled back the curtain a little bit, and there was a baby brother. "But hold on," the father said with a smile.

He pulled back the curtain a little bit farther—and there was *another* baby brother. But he wasn't finished yet. He pulled it back even farther, and there was a third baby brother!

"Now," the dad said, "aren't you glad you prayed?"

"Yes," the boy replied. "But aren't you glad I stopped after three months?"

We all go through seasons when we wonder if our prayers are getting through or just ricocheting off the ceiling. It's discouraging, isn't it?

When we don't see results in our lives or the lives of others, why should we keep praying?

Part of the answer lies in understanding the unimaginable *power* that God has made available to us as His sons and daughters.

God Has Deposited His Power in Us

This is extremely important to understand. When you finally understand this about prayer, you will become a person of prayer, and it will help you understand how and why we pray—and why we keep praying, even when we don't yet see results. In Luke 24:49 we read these words from Jesus to His disciples:

> Behold, I send the Promise of My Father upon you; but tarry in the city of Jerusalem until you are endued with [or receive] power from on high.

In Acts 1:8, Jesus essentially repeats that promise, "But you shall receive power when the Holy Spirit has come upon you." He is telling the disciples they will have power deposited in them once He leaves the earth.

And that's only the beginning of the story. Paul expands on that idea in Ephesians 3:20 when he writes: "Now to Him who is able to do *exceedingly abundantly above all* that we ask or think, according to the power that works [or resides] in us" (emphasis mine).

It's amazing how the Holy Spirit structured this verse. You have to understand that He could have left out the three adverbs—*exceedingly*, *abundantly*, and *above*—and the verse would have meant basically the same thing:

"God is able to do all that we ask or think."

But apparently, the Holy Spirit didn't think that statement described God's ability adequately, so He put the word *above* in front of the word *all*:

God is able to do both *all* and *above all*.

But somehow even that description wasn't enough. So the Holy Spirit added the word *abundantly* before the words *above all*.

God is able to do *abundantly above all* that we ask or think.

But that still didn't capture it. So God's Spirit inserted the word *exceedingly* before the word *abundantly*.

As a result, the verse extravagantly describes the fulfillment of Jesus' promise. The power that God has deposited in us is "exceedingly, abundantly, above all we ask or think."

Is that your experience in your life, in your immediate situation—that God is able to do exceedingly abundantly above all that you can ask or even imagine? Can that actually happen?

Absolutely! Since God's Word is true, and we know He can't lie, He certainly is able to do these things.

We all go through *seasons*
when we wonder if our prayers
are getting through or just
ricocheting off the *ceiling*.

Ephesians 3:20 extravagantly
describes the fulfillment of
Jesus' promise. The power
that God has deposited
in us is "exceedingly,
abundantly, above all
we ask or think."

Then why doesn't He?

That's the question, isn't it? In my life, in my marriage, in my family, in my health, in this situation I'm going through right now . . . if God is able to make such a difference, then why in the world doesn't He do it?

That last phrase suggests the answer: "according to the power that works in us." The word translated as "according to" is the Greek word *kata*, which can carry a sense of "measuring out" or distribution.

So here is a very simple question.

How much of God's limitless power are you measuring out into your life? Into your family? Into your job or mission field?

How much of God's power are you distributing to the situation in which you need God to work right now?

Is it possible that He has already done His part and deposited His power in you and now it is your responsibility to measure it out and distribute it?

Obviously, we are weak human beings, hardly more than microscopic dust specks in God's vast universe. We pray to God because He is the Source of all power, all wisdom, all authority. Before Him . . .

> *the nations are like a drop in the bucket;*
> *they are regarded as dust on the scales. . . .*
> *He sits enthroned above the circle of the earth,*
> *and its people are like grasshoppers.*
> *He stretches out the heavens like a canopy,*
> *and spreads them out like a tent to live in.*
>
> Isaiah 40:15, 22 NIV

We know these things about the might and authority of our God. He is the power behind every answered prayer anyone has ever prayed.

And yet . . . God has chosen to distribute His power through our prayers! The question is, will we—in His perfect timing—receive and measure out His might, goodness, and grace into our lives, our families, and our world?

We Must Release His Power Through Prayer

In the gospel of John, we read this account of a very significant day in our Lord's life:

> On the last day, that great day of the feast, Jesus stood and cried out, saying, "If anyone thirsts, let him come to Me and drink. He who believes in Me, as the Scripture has said, out of his heart will flow rivers of living water." But this He spoke concerning the Spirit, whom those believing in Him would receive; for the Holy Spirit was not yet given, because Jesus was not yet glorified. (John 7:37–39)

The feast John speaks of in this passage was an eight-day feast in Jerusalem called the Feast of the Tabernacles. For seven of those eight days the people took part in what was called a "water ceremony" or "water libation," when the high priest took water from the Pool of Siloam and poured it

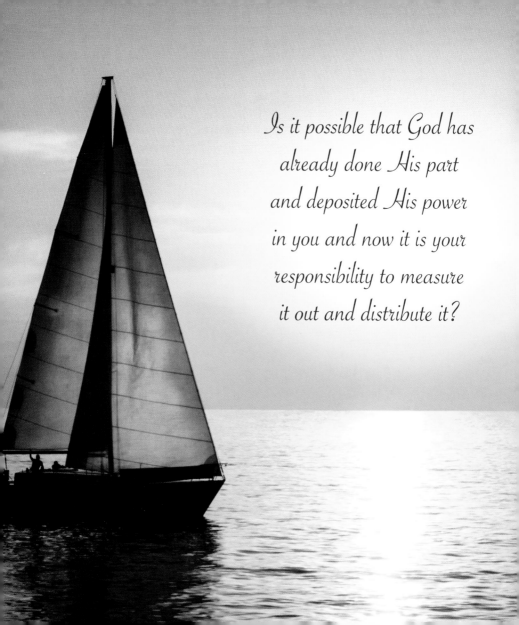

Is it possible that God has
already done His part
and deposited His power
in you and now it is your
responsibility to measure
it out and distribute it?

onto the altar while the people chanted prayers. This practice grew out of one occurrence and one prophecy in the Old Testament.

When the people of Israel were going through the wilderness, God instructed Moses on two occasions to bring water from the rock to satisfy the needs of the thirsty people. On the first occasion he was to strike the rock, and on the second occasion he was to speak to the rock. Each time, water came gushing out of sheer stone, and the people always referred to that as "living water."

Later, the prophet Zechariah foresaw a future day when living water would once again flow out of Jerusalem:

> *And in that day it shall be*
> *That living waters shall flow from Jerusalem,*
> *Half of them toward the eastern sea*
> *And half of them toward the western sea;*
> *In both summer and winter it shall occur.*
> *And the LORD shall be King over all the earth. (14:8–9)*

So the people of Israel gathered in Jerusalem for an eight-day feast, and for seven days they prayed for living water from heaven. Then, on the eighth day, they prayed for rain.

Now, it's not wrong to pray for rain. Where I live in Texas, in the dry southwestern part of our country, we find ourselves doing that all the time. But the way the people of Israel were praying wasn't right. In essence, what they were saying was, "We will pray for living water from God, but if we can't get it, we'll just take natural water."

You see, the whole feast in those days had become something of a religious formality, and the prayers were mostly for show, not something the people were praying from their hearts. Many would even get drunk and commit immoral acts during the course of the eight-day feast.

On the occasion described in John 7, the people had just finished going through the motions of praying for living water when Jesus suddenly stood up and spoke in a loud voice: "If anyone thirsts, let him come to Me and drink" (v. 37).

In other words, "Listen to Me. I am the answer to your

prayers. Every year you gather at this time and pray for something to quench your thirst. Now here I am, standing before you, and if you are truly thirsty, you're invited to come and drink. You will find the Living Water that you seek."

Then Jesus made this statement: "He who believes in Me . . . out of his heart will flow rivers of living water" (v. 38). And John tells us that at that moment Jesus was speaking of the Holy Spirit. Later, of course, He would say it more explicitly: "But you shall receive power when the Holy Spirit has come upon you" (Acts 1:8).

And what will the Holy Spirit do when He comes upon you in power?

He will flow out of your heart.

So here is my question for you: How wide is your river? Is it a gushing flow or just a trickle? How much power—the Holy Spirit's power—is flowing out of you? And what does this have to do with how you pray?

Is it possible that you have your hand on the faucet of God's power in your life? Are you asking God to simply release the power He has already deposited within you?

Let the Faucet Run

The fact is, many of us have more faith in our hot-water faucets than we do in prayer. We turn the handle and wait for the stream of water to become hot. Sometimes we may wait so long we find ourselves wondering if the water heater was installed at the neighbor's three houses down. But do you know what? We may be impatient at times, but we don't doubt the hot water will eventually come.

But too often, when we pray, we give up way too soon. We turn on the prayer faucet, and we gauge the results based on the temperature of the "water." But if we don't see results right away, we become impatient, distracted, or preoccupied and turn off the faucet again. We stop praying instead of hanging on to the assurance that if we would simply leave that faucet on, eventually the water will become hot.

To become a conduit of the power promised to us, we have to let the faucet run. We have to pray—and keep praying.

That's what the widow in Luke 18 did. That's what many other believing men and women in Scripture did. They prayed and prayed, knowing that the cold would eventually become hot.

"You shall receive power when the Holy Spirit has come upon you."

Acts 1:8

To become a **conduit** of the *power* promised to us, we have to let the faucet **run**. We have to pray— and **keep praying**.

Why, for instance, did Elijah climb to the top of Mount Carmel, bend himself down to the ground, and put his face between his knees, praying seven times for the Lord to bring rain? (1 Kings 18: 42–44).

God had already told Elijah that He would send badly needed rain on the earth (v. 1). Elijah could have said, "Well, if God said it will happen, it will happen. I'll just sit back and watch."

But Elijah didn't do that. Instead, he bowed himself low and prayed. Then he prayed again. And he kept on praying—seven times.

But why? If God said He would do it, why did Elijah have to pray? For that matter, why did Elijah have to pray seven times and not just once?

Could it be that he was waiting for God's living water to be unleashed?

Daniel prayed for twenty-one days as he sought to understand the significance of the visions God had given to him. Scripture says that during those three weeks he consumed no choice foods, no meat, and no wine. He prayed and prayed some more. And then, after three weeks, he looked up and saw he had an angelic visitor, who said,

"Do not be afraid, Daniel. Since the first day that you set your mind to gain understanding and to humble yourself before your God, your words were heard, and I have come in response to them. But the prince of the Persian kingdom resisted me twenty-one days. Then Michael, one of the chief princes, came to help me, because I was detained there with the king of Persia." (Daniel 10:12–13 NIV)

This awesome, powerful angel was saying, "Daniel, the very first day you prayed, I left heaven with your answer. But there's a war in the heavens, and I couldn't get through at first. But you kept praying, and I was able to get through."

What was true in Daniel's day is true in ours as well. War still rages in the heavenly realms. Ephesians 6:12 tells us that "we do not wrestle against flesh and blood" and that there are "spiritual hosts of wickedness in the heavenly places."

So we don't always know what is going on behind the scenes while we wrestle and pray and—from our perspective—wait for something to happen.

But I want you to understand something. *The answer is sent on the first day that we pray.* The power of God is released. We just need to keep the prayer faucet running until the answer is received and the living water starts to flow.

In other words, we need to keep on praying.

What if Daniel had given up after twenty days? Would there have been an answer on the twenty-first day?

Moving Power from Heaven to Earth

Think about it like this: How much of the work of our salvation has been done? The answer, of course, is *all of it.* Now, it may not be "done" in every person's life, because some have yet to open their hearts to receive it. But everything that God needed to do, everything that Christ set out to accomplish, has already been completed. Jesus will never die on the cross again. His work is complete. It is finished. But if we want to enter into that finished work, there is something we need to do. We need to receive that offer of salvation.

Could that truth have a parallel to our prayer life?

Could it be that what you have been praying about has already been done in heaven, but you need to help move it from heaven to earth?

The book of Ephesians tells us that we have been blessed "with every spiritual blessing in the heavenly places in Christ" (1:3).

How many spiritual blessings have you received?

All of them. Every one of them.

Why then, don't we see all of this at work in our lives? Because we have to move it from heaven to earth. The work has already been done as far as God is concerned. The question is, how will we respond to it?

We must release His power through our prayers.

God Adds His Fire to Our Prayers

In the book of Revelation, we encounter this amazing scene:

> Now when He had taken the scroll, the four living creatures and the twenty-four elders fell down before the Lamb, each having a harp, and golden bowls full of incense, which are the prayers of the saints. (5:8)

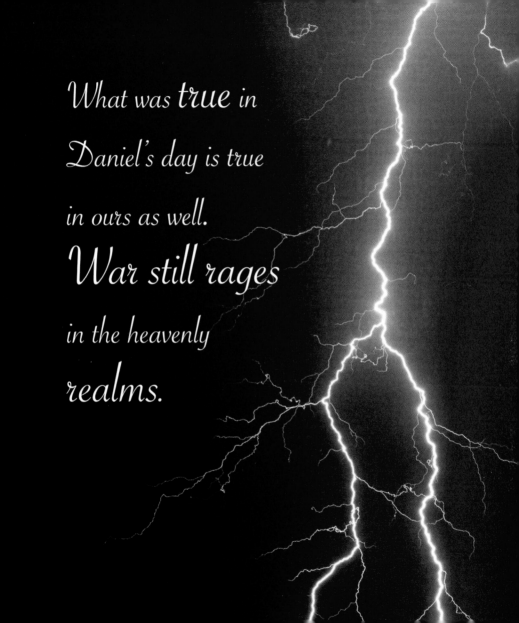

What was true in Daniel's day is true in ours as well. War still rages in the heavenly realms.

Then, a few pages later we read this:

> And I saw the seven angels who stand before God, and to
> them were given seven trumpets. Then another angel, hav-
> ing a golden censer, came and stood at the altar. He was given
> much incense, that he should offer it with the prayers of all
> the saints upon the golden altar which was before the throne.
> And the smoke of the incense, with the prayers of the saints,
> ascended before God from the angel's hand. Then the angel
> took the censer, filled it with fire from the altar, and threw
> it to the earth. And there were noises, thunderings, light-
> nings, and an earthquake. (Revelation 8:2–5)

Just picture that scene in your mind. Visualize that array
of golden bowls in heaven, each filled to the brim with the
prayers of God's people. Imagine the fragrant incense from
those prayers ascending to God's throne. And then picture
an angel whose job it is to add fire from the altar—God's
fire—to those prayers of ours and throw them back down to
the earth.

How many
spiritual blessings
have you received?
All of them.
Every one of them.

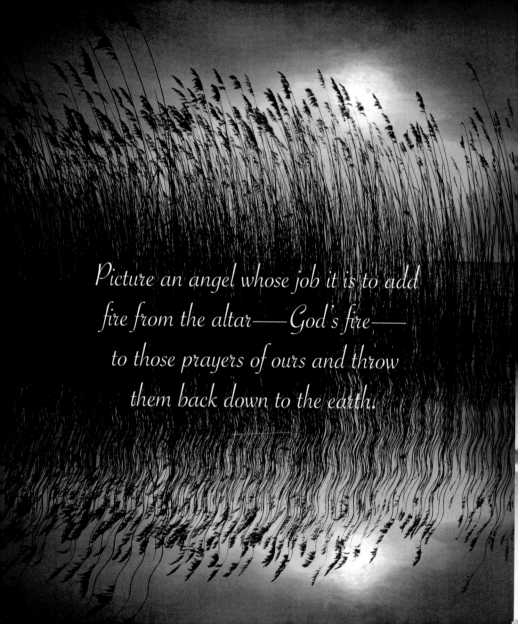

Picture an angel whose job it is to add
fire from the altar——God's fire——
to those prayers of ours and throw
them back down to the earth.

This is the same fire that kindled the bush in the Midian desert (Exodus 3).

This is the same fire that went before the people of Israel in a great pillar as they came out of Egypt (Exodus 13:21–22).

This is the same fire that rained down on Mount Carmel and defeated the prophets of Baal (1 Kings 18:20–40).

This is the same fire that fell on the day of Pentecost (Acts 2:1–4).

This is the fire of God and the power of God. And according to Revelation, it's directly connected with prayer.

With that in mind, I have a very simple question: How full are your prayer bowls?

You have said you need to pray for your friend who needs Jesus. That's good. *How full is that prayer bowl?*

You've felt the need to pray for your spouse and your marriage. *Is that bowl filled to the brim?*

You have a health concern that troubles your thoughts, and you know God invites you to pray about that concern. *Does that bowl have a little inside, or is it spilling over?*

How much time have you spent in prayer over these areas

of your life—or others? If you could actually see those bowls in heaven with your physical eyes, as John did, how full would they be? How much have you put into them? And what happens when they get so full that they spill over?

I'm visualizing in my mind one of those garden fountains made up of a succession of bowls. Have you seen one? The top bowl gets full to the very brim and then suddenly tips over, spilling into the bowl below and filling it up. But the bowl doesn't tip until it's full.

How full are your prayer bowls? Could it be that there's an angel of God assigned to watch them? Could it be that when one of them gets full, he adds fire from God's altar and throws it back to the earth?

That is when things change.

That is when events beyond expectation begin to happen.

Do miracles still happen? Of course they do—every hour and every day. But some miracles take longer than others . . . as our own family discovered.

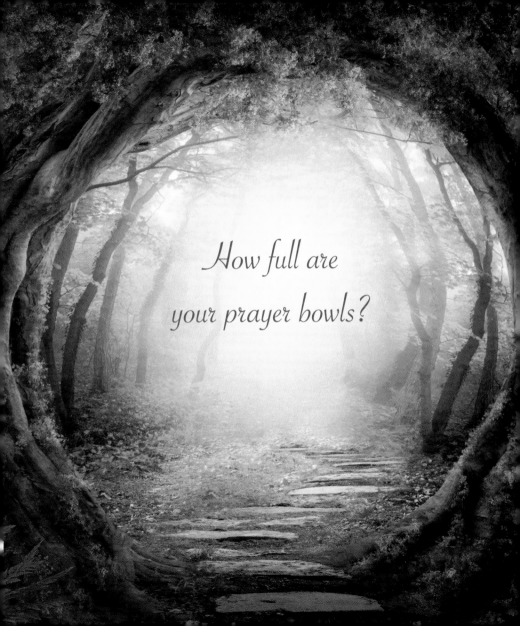

There was a man named Ray Alexander who prayed for my grandfather, Joe Morris, for forty years.

During one period of his life, my grandfather worked for the Texas Department of Transportation. His job was to put asphalt in potholes, and he and Ray worked side by side for a number of weeks.

Ray was a Christian, and he shared Christ with my grandfather, who didn't know anything about the Lord. One day my grandfather said, "I'd like to hear more about this." So Ray said to him, "Why don't you come to my house after dinner? I'll share with you some more and show you some verses from the Bible."

My grandfather agreed to that. So that night after dinner, he got ready to go to Ray's house.

Now my grandfather's son, my father, had just turned sixteen and was in possession of a brand-new driver's license.

"Where are you going?" he asked his dad.

"A man at work wanted to talk to me," he replied, "and I'm going over to his place."

"Can I drive you?" my father asked. (Any excuse to get behind the wheel!)

"Yes," my grandfather said, "but you have to stay outside while we talk."

"That's okay."

So my dad drove my grandfather over to Ray Alexander's house, and Dad sat on the front porch steps while the men inside were talking. There was no air conditioning in those days, so the front door was open, but the screen door was closed. My dad could hear the whole conversation between the two men inside, and that evening, at sixteen years of age, he heard the gospel for the first time. No one had ever told him that Jesus was the Son of God and that He had left heaven to die on a cross for my dad's sins, so that he could live forever in heaven.

As the conversation was wrapping up, Ray Alexander said to my grandfather, "Joe, would you like to accept Jesus as your Lord and Savior?"

"No," he replied slowly. "No, not now. I'd like to think about it for a while."

"Well," Ray told him, "if you ever do decide to give your life to Jesus, you need to pray a prayer like this . . ." And slowly and carefully, he told my grandfather the sinner's prayer.

Unbeknownst to either of them, my father, sitting on the porch, heard that prayer through the screen door and prayed it himself, giving his life to the Lord.

My dad was the oldest of three sons. One of his brothers later committed suicide, and the other died a few months after getting out of prison. My father was the only believer in his whole family. Soon after he received Christ as his Savior, he went off to college—the first one in the family to ever do so. After college he started a company, and God blessed him. He became a man who invested a great deal of money in the kingdom of God. He raised me in a Christian home where I accepted the Lord, eventually heading into the ministry.

Through all the years of my pastoral ministry, many, many people have accepted the Lord as Savior . . . because a man who put asphalt in potholes shared the gospel with another man. And as far as he ever knew, that other man had said no to his message.

A few years after I came to know the Lord, I became concerned about my grandfather and started praying for him. We had a family reunion coming up, and I prayed I'd get a chance

Unbeknownst to either of them, my father, sitting on the porch, heard that prayer through the screen door and prayed it himself,

to talk to him about the Lord. In answer to that prayer, God orchestrated a time for the two of us to be alone in a room, and I began to tell him about my relationship with Jesus.

My grandfather seemed to really be listening. After a while he looked up at me with sadness in his eyes. "A man told me all this forty years ago," he said. "His name was Ray. Ray Alexander. And you know, I've always regretted that I didn't give my life to the Lord."

"You can give your life to the Lord today," I told him. "You can do it right now."

And there, in that room, I led my grandfather to the Lord. He was seventy-eight years old at the time, and he lived until the age of eighty-two. I was privileged to witness the change in his life during those last four years.

After my grandfather passed away, I thought to myself, *I wonder if this Ray Alexander is still alive.* I felt like I needed to call him. And as it turned out, he wasn't that difficult to find. He still lived in the same town, and all I had to do was call directory assistance to get his phone number. (That's how we used to find people before the Internet.)

Ray Alexander, now eighty-one years old, answered the phone. I said to him, "Do you remember a man named Joe Morris?"

He replied without hesitation. "Yes, I do," he said. "In fact, I still pray for him to this day."

"I'm his grandson," I explained. "Did you realize that my dad accepted Christ on your front porch as you shared the gospel with my grandfather?"

"I didn't know that," he said, and he began to cry.

I told him then that my grandfather, too, had received Jesus before he died. "I'm a minister," I said, "and there have been many, many people who have come to the Lord through the years. But it's all because you shared the gospel with my grandfather—and my father—on that evening."

The old man couldn't speak. He was overcome with emotion.

"Mr. Alexander," I said, "you said that you still pray for my grandfather to this day. Why do you still pray for him?"

"In the back of my Bible," he explained, "I have all of the names of the men I've shared Christ with. I pray for every man until he accepts Christ. When he accepts Christ, I put a check by his name. Your grandfather was the only name in the back of my

Bible that didn't have a check beside it. When I get off the phone, I'm going to put a check mark beside your grandfather's name."

Prayer works.

So don't ever give up.

Don't leave that prayer bowl half filled. Fill it up until it spills over.

Fill it up until it's charged with the power of God.

What do you need to pray about right now? Are you in a season of life when it seems like nothing is going to change? Are you deeply concerned about someone in your life who needs a touch from God—or an outright rescue? In what area of your life do you need to see the power of God released?

It will never happen if you shrug your shoulders and walk away.

Remember, He is the God who is able to do "exceedingly abundantly above all" that we could ask or think. In other words, His answers to your faithful, persistent prayers could very well go beyond your wildest dreams or imaginations.

Trust Him. Keep praying!

Lord, You have given us a glimpse of the mysteries of heaven, and we won't forget it. We may not understand very much about what it means to fill up bowls of prayer in Your presence, but we know that it's important, or You would have never given us that picture at all. Lord, help us now to be faithful, to hold on to our hope and faith in You, and to pray and pray through the days, weeks, and years of our lives . . . until the bowls fill up, spill over, and Your fire falls where it might not have ever fallen if we had neglected to pray.

In Jesus' name we pray, amen.

Pray always, and don't give up.

An Invitation to Pray

I f you received an invitation from a highly respected person of influence to come by his or her house for coffee or to go for a walk along the river trail for some conversation, you would probably respond with eagerness and anticipation. You wouldn't lightly discard it. And if you received two or three invitations, you would be amazed.

But what if you received a thousand invitations? Or one every day for the rest of your life?

Come to Me. Come soon. Come anytime. Come as you are. The door's open. I am waiting for you. Let's make time to be together. Let's open our hearts to one another.

The Bible, from beginning to end, offers hundreds upon hundreds of invitations for us to approach the God of the

Universe—to be with Him, to draw close to Him, to receive guidance and comfort, to praise and worship Him, and to simply share what's on our hearts with Him. In many voices and in countless ways—in whispers, shouts, commands, and gentle words—God makes it clear in His Word that He wants close, intimate conversation.

And He wants it with *you*.

God is near, and He's ready to listen. Meet with Him and open your heart in prayer . . .

> *"Call to Me, and I will answer you, and show you great and mighty things, which you do not know."*
>
> ⟿ JEREMIAH 33:3

> *If any of you lacks wisdom, let him ask of God, who gives to all liberally and without reproach, and it will be given to him. But let him ask in faith, with no doubting, for he who doubts is like a wave of the sea driven and tossed by the wind.*
>
> ⟿ JAMES 1:5–6

"If My people who are called by My name will humble themselves, and pray and seek My face, and turn from their wicked ways, then I will hear from heaven, and will forgive their sin and heal their land."

~ 2 Chronicles 7:14

"Because he loves me," says the Lord, "I will rescue him; I will protect him, for he acknowledges my name. He will call on me, and I will answer him; I will be with him in trouble, I will deliver him and honor him. With long life I will satisfy him and show him my salvation."

~ Psalm 91:14–16 NIV

"Ask, and it will be given to you; seek, and you will find; knock, and it will be opened to you."

~ Matthew 7:7

Prayers of Praise

Lord, you alone are my portion and my cup;
you make my lot secure.
The boundary lines have fallen for me in pleasant
  places;
surely I have a delightful inheritance.
I will praise the Lord, who counsels me;
even at night my heart instructs me.
I keep my eyes always on the Lord.
With him at my right hand, I will not be shaken. . . .
You make known to me the path of life;
you will fill me with joy in your presence,
with eternal pleasures at your right hand.

⌐ Psalm 16:5–8, 11 NIV

"Father, I thank You that You have heard Me. And I
know that You always hear Me."

⌐ JOHN 11:41–42

You have searched me, Lord,
and you know me.
You know when I sit and when I rise;
you perceive my thoughts from afar.
You discern my going out and my lying down;
you are familiar with all my ways.
Before a word is on my tongue
you, LORD, know it completely.
You hem me in behind and before,
and you lay your hand upon me.
Such knowledge is too wonderful for me,
too lofty for me to attain.

~ Psalm 139:1–6 NIV

O God, You are my God;
Early will I seek You;
My soul thirsts for You;
My flesh longs for You
In a dry and thirsty land
Where there is no water.

So I have looked for You in the sanctuary,
To see Your power and Your glory.

Because Your lovingkindness is better than life,
My lips shall praise You.
Thus I will bless You while I live;
I will lift up my hands in Your name.
My soul shall be satisfied as with marrow and fatness,
And my mouth shall praise You with joyful lips.

When I remember You on my bed,
I meditate on You in the night watches.
Because You have been my help,
Therefore in the shadow of Your wings I will rejoice.
My soul follows close behind You;
Your right hand upholds me.

~ Psalm 63:1–8

Prayers for Mercy and Grace

"God, have mercy on me, a sinner."

～ LUKE 18:13 NIV

Remember, O Lord, Your tender mercies and Your
*   lovingkindnesses,*
For they are from of old.
Do not remember the sins of my youth, nor my
*   transgressions;*
According to Your mercy remember me,
For Your goodness' sake, O Lord.

～ Psalm 25:6–7

I call on you, my God, for you will answer me;
turn your ear to me and hear my prayer.
Show me the wonders of your great love,
you who save by your right hand . . .
Keep me as the apple of your eye;
hide me in the shadow of your wings.

～ Psalm 17:6–8 NIV

Prayers for Times of Doubt

Lord, I believe; help my unbelief!

~ MARK 9:24

*Yea, though I walk through the valley of the shadow of
    death,*
I will fear no evil;
For You are with me;
Your rod and Your staff, they comfort me.
*You prepare a table before me in the presence of my
    enemies;*
You anoint my head with oil;
My cup runs over.
Surely goodness and mercy shall follow me
All the days of my life;
And I will dwell in the house of the LORD
Forever.

~ Psalm 23:4–6

As for me, my feet had almost slipped;
I had nearly lost my foothold.
For I envied the arrogant
when I saw the prosperity of the wicked. . . .
Yet I am always with you;
you hold me by my right hand.
You guide me with your counsel,
and afterward you will take me into glory.
Whom have I in heaven but you?
And earth has nothing I desire besides you.

~ Psalm 73:2–3, 23–25 NIV

Prayers for Guidance

Search me, God, and know my heart;
test me and know my anxious thoughts.
See if there is any offensive way in me,
and lead me in the way everlasting.

~ Psalm 139:23–24 NIV

To You, O Lord, I lift up my soul.
O my God, I trust in You;
Let me not be ashamed;
Let not my enemies triumph over me.
Indeed, let no one who waits on You be ashamed;
Let those be ashamed who deal treacherously without
  cause.
Show me Your ways, O Lord;
Teach me Your paths.
Lead me in Your truth and teach me,
For You are the God of my salvation;
On You I wait all the day.

~ Psalm 25:1–5

Teach me to do your will,
for you are my God;
may your good Spirit
lead me on level ground.

~ Psalm 143:10 NIV

Send me your light and your faithful care,
let them lead me;
let them bring me to your holy mountain,
to the place where you dwell.

~ Psalm 43:3 NIV

Prayers for When You are Afraid

Lord, do not forsake me;
do not be far from me, my God.
Come quickly to help me,
my Lord and my Savior.

~ Psalm 38:21–22 NIV

Protect me, for I am devoted to you.
Save me, for I serve you and trust you.
You are my God.

~ Psalm 86:2 NLT

Whenever I am afraid,
I will trust in You. . . .
You number my wanderings;
Put my tears into Your bottle;
Are they not in Your book?
When I cry out to You,
Then my enemies will turn back;
This I know, because God is for me.
In God (I will praise His word),
In the Lord (I will praise His word),
In God I have put my trust;
I will not be afraid.
What can man do to me?

~ Psalm 56:3, 8–11

I will both lie down in peace, and sleep;
For You alone, O LORD, make me dwell in safety.

~ Psalm 4:8

Fear not, for I am with you;
Be not dismayed, for I am your God.
I will strengthen you,
Yes, I will help you,
I will uphold you with My righteous right hand.

⁓ Isaiah 41:10

Verses for Strength

My health may fail, and my spirit may grow weak,
but God remains the strength of my heart;
he is mine forever.

⁓ Psalm 73:26 NLT

The Lord is faithful, and he will strengthen and
protect you from the evil one.

⁓ 2 THESSALONIANS 3:3 NIV

In you, Lord, I have taken refuge;
let me never be put to shame;
deliver me in your righteousness.
Turn your ear to me,
come quickly to my rescue;
be my rock of refuge,
a strong fortress to save me.
Since you are my rock and my fortress,
for the sake of your name lead and guide me.
Keep me free from the trap that is set for me,
for you are my refuge.
Into your hands I commit my spirit;
deliver me, Lord, my faithful God.

　　　　　　　　　　　　～ Psalm 31:1–5 NIV

For the eyes of the Lord range throughout the earth to
strengthen those whose hearts are fully committed to
him.

　　　　　　　　　　　　～ 2 Chronicles 16:9 NIV

And the God of all grace, who called you to his
eternal glory in Christ . . . will himself restore you
and make you strong, firm, and steadfast.

〜 1 PETER 5:10 NIV

Prayers for Blessings

"O LORD, God of heaven, the great and awesome
God who keeps his covenant of unfailing love with
those who love him and obey his commands, listen
to my prayer! . . . Please grant me success today."

〜 NEHEMIAH 1:5–6, 11 NLT

O LORD God of hosts, hear my prayer;
Give ear, O God of Jacob! Selah
O God, behold our shield,
And look upon the face of Your anointed.

For a day in Your courts is better than a thousand.
I would rather be a doorkeeper in the house of my God
Than dwell in the tents of wickedness.
For the LORD God is a sun and shield;
The LORD will give grace and glory;
No good thing will He withhold
From those who walk uprightly.

O LORD of hosts,
Blessed is the man who trusts in You!

~ Psalm 84:8–12

Oh, that you would bless me and enlarge my
territory! Let your hand be with me, and keep me
from harm so that I will be free from pain.

~ THE PRAYER OF JABEZ, 1 CHRONICLES 4:10 NIV

Now therefore, I pray, if I have found grace in Your sight, show me now Your way, that I may know You and that I may find grace in Your sight.

∽ MOSES' PRAYER, EXODUS 33:13

Jesus' Prayer for All Believers

"Righteous Father, though the world does not know you, I know you, and they know that you have sent me. I have made you known to them, and will continue to make you known in order that the love you have for me may be in them and that I myself may be in them."

∽ JOHN 17:25–26 NIV

Prayers for Troubled Times

Hear me, LORD, and answer me,
for I am poor and needy.
Guard my life, for I am faithful to you;
save your servant who trusts in you.
You are my God; have mercy on me, Lord,
for I call to you all day long.
Bring joy to your servant, Lord,
for I put my trust in you.
You, Lord, are forgiving and good,
abounding in love to all who call to you.
Hear my prayer, LORD;
listen to my cry for mercy.
When I am in distress, I call to you,
because you answer me.

For you are great and do marvelous deeds;
you alone are God.

⌒ Psalm 86:1–7, 10 NIV

Return, O LORD, deliver me!
Oh, save me for Your mercies' sake!

~ Psalm 6:4

For You will light my lamp;
The LORD my God will enlighten my darkness.

~ Psalm 18:28

But as for me, I trust in You, O LORD;
I say, "You are my God."
My times are in Your hand.

~ Psalm 31:14–15

Give heed to the voice of my cry,
My King and my God,
For to You I will pray.
My voice You shall hear in the morning, O LORD;
In the morning I will direct it to You. . . .
Lead me, O LORD, in Your righteousness because of my enemies;
Make Your way straight before my face.

~ Psalm 5:2–3, 8

LORD, *how they have increased who trouble me!*
Many are they who rise up against me.
Many are they who say of me,
"There is no help for him in God."
But You, O LORD, *are a shield for me,*
My glory and the One who lifts up my head.
I cried to the LORD *with my voice,*
And He heard me from His holy hill.

~ Psalm 3:1–4

Notes

1. Priscilla Van Sutphin, "The Unjust Judge," *Upstream Ministries*, March 28, 2008, www.upstreamca.org/unjustjudge.html.
2. Billy Graham, quoted in Beliefnet's Inspirational Quotes, Beliefnet, http://www.beliefnet.com/Quotes/Christian/B/Billy-Graham/The -Christian-Life-Is-Not-A-Constant-High-I-Have.aspx?

What Is Keeping You From
Being Truly Free?

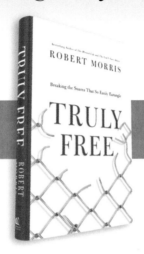

In his best seller *The Blessed Life*, Pastor Robert Morris transformed our perspective on giving. Now, in *Truly Free*, he offers us a powerful new way of looking at spiritual freedom.

AVAILABLE WHEREVER BOOKS AND EBOOKS ARE SOLD.

"Robert Morris has a remarkable way of knowing where I live and helping me move forward. I love him and his teaching."

—Max Lucado